THE GREAT GATSBY

"Owen Davis's play *The Great Gatsby*, which had a successful Broadway run in 1926, reimagined and even recast Fitzgerald's book in ways that gave it resonance both as an expression of the Roaring Twenties zeitgeist, and after, as an approach to the ways the novel, in a new form, still tells *the* American story. With Anne Margaret Daniel and James L. W. West III's perceptive and instructive introduction providing context, this engrossing script has its own story to tell and insights to Fitzgerald to reveal. And like the novel, it cuts to the heart of America."

Linda Patterson Miller,
Distinguished Professor of English, Penn State Abington

"Owen Davis's stage dramatization of Fitzgerald's novel is, in more ways than one, a peep behind the scenes at Gatsby's life. Davis rearranged dialogue and chronology, while sticking to the familiar story — rather in the manner of a jazz musician improvising on a standard. His hero is closer to bootlegger Gatz than playboy Gatsby. Anne Margaret Daniel and James L. W. West III have unearthed a fascinating curiosity. Their introduction provides just the right amount of confidential information the audience needs, before the play begins."

James Campbell, author of
Talking at the Gates: A Life of James Baldwin

"With Anne Margaret Daniel's 2022 Norton Library edition and James L. W. West III's 2019 variorum edition, this book's editors have each given us a superlative edition of *The Great Gatsby*. Together, they have done the same for the Broadway play adapted from it. *The Great Gatsby: The 1926 Broadway Script* will interest anyone who likes *The Great Gatsby* and fascinate anyone who loves it."

Scott Jordan Harris, author of
Rosebud Sleds and Horses' Heads:
50 of Film's Most Evocative Objects

"Short of discovering a portal to the past or building a time machine, readers will never come closer to returning to Broadway's Jazz Age heyday than with this edition of Owen Davis's 1926 theatrical adaptation of *The Great Gatsby*. Masterfully edited by Anne Margaret Daniel and James L. W. West III, Davis's script channels the melancholy spirit of Fitzgerald's classic while making the changes necessary for the tragic story of American aspiration to succeed on the stage, allowing us to appreciate why the show ran for more than 100 performances."

Kirk Curnutt, executive director,
the F. Scott Fitzgerald Society

"Gatsby has a gangster gang, 'Buck' Wilson is his chauffeur, Daisy and Myrtle meet at a party. This is not the novel but the playscript of the hit 1926 Broadway production of *The Great Gatsby*, and it's a great read. Daniel and West have a major coup here with this edition. Bravo for their fascinating introduction, generous readers' notes, and deep research."

William Blažek, vice president,
the F. Scott Fitzgerald Society

"This edition of the 1926 Broadway script of *The Great Gatsby* by Owen Davis is a treasure on many counts. The play achieves the near-magical feat of capturing the soul of Fitzgerald's novel — even in spite of the fact that Davis extensively altered major details of the story. Its publication by Cambridge on the eve of the centennial of the first publication of the novel renders it an indispensable companion volume to Fitzgerald's masterpiece."

Bryant Mangum, editor, *F. Scott Fitzgerald in Context*

"Meticulously edited by James L. W. West III and Anne Margaret Daniel, this authoritative edition of the 1926 stage adaptation of *The Great Gatsby* does more than fill a surprising gap in the scholarly canon. The play will also be entertaining and enlightening for students of the novel and the period — some may well judge it superior to many of the adaptations that have followed it. An essential contribution to Fitzgerald studies."

Sarah Churchwell,
Professor of American Literature,
School of Advanced Study, University of London

"The Final Pot Shot at The Great Gatsby." Illustration by Miguel Covarrubias.

THE GREAT GATSBY

THE 1926 BROADWAY SCRIPT
BY OWEN DAVIS

BASED UPON THE NOVEL BY
F. SCOTT FITZGERALD

EDITED BY

ANNE MARGARET DANIEL

AND

JAMES L. W. WEST III

CAMBRIDGE
UNIVERSITY PRESS

Shaftesbury Road, Cambridge CB2 8EA, United Kingdom

One Liberty Plaza, 20th Floor, New York, NY 10006, USA

477 Williamstown Road, Port Melbourne, VIC 3207, Australia

314–321, 3rd Floor, Plot 3, Splendor Forum, Jasola District Centre,
New Delhi – 110025, India

103 Penang Road, #05–06/07, Visioncrest Commercial, Singapore 238467

Cambridge University Press is part of Cambridge University Press & Assessment,
a department of the University of Cambridge.

We share the University's mission to contribute to society through the pursuit of
education, learning and research at the highest international levels of excellence.

www.cambridge.org
Information on this title: www.cambridge.org/9781009385220

DOI: 10.1017/9781009377508

© Cambridge University Press & Assessment 2024

First published 2024

The script of the 1926 production of *The Great Gatsby* passed
into the public domain on January 1, 2022.

An early version of the introduction appears in James L. W. West III,
Business Is Good: F. Scott Fitzgerald, Professional Author (University
Park, PA: Pennsylvania State University Press, 2023): 32-58.

Printed in the United Kingdom by TJ Books Limited, Padstow, Cornwall

A catalogue record for this publication is available from the British Library.

Library of Congress Cataloging-in-Publication Data
Names: Davis, Owen, 1874–1956 author. | Fitzgerald, F. Scott (Francis
Scott), 1896–1940. Great Gatsby. | West, James L. W., III editor. |
Daniel, Anne Margaret, 1963– editor.
Title: The Great Gatsby : the 1926 Broadway script : based upon the novel
by F. Scott Fitzgerald / edited by Anne Margaret Daniel and James L. W.
West III.
Description: New York : Cambridge University Press, 2024.
Identifiers: LCCN 2023044521 | ISBN 9781009385220 (hardback) | ISBN
9781009377492 (paperback) | ISBN 9781009377508 (epub)
Subjects: LCGFT: Drama.
Classification: LCC PS3507.A745 G74 2024 | DDC 812/.52–dc23/eng/20231102
LC record available at https://lccn.loc.gov/2023044521

ISBN 978-1-009-38522-0 Hardback

CONTENTS

ILLUSTRATIONS

Frontispiece and illustrations 8 and 13 are from Scrapbook IV, Fitzgerald Papers, Princeton University Library.
Illustrations 2–7 and 9–12 are from the collections of the New York Public Library for the Performing Arts.

ACKNOWLEDGMENTS

We are grateful to the staff of the Manuscripts Division, Department of Rare Books and Special Collections, Princeton University Library, for assistance with the Broadway script and with other materials from the F. Scott Fitzgerald Papers. For supplying a copy of the Broadway script from the Owen Davis collection, we thank the American Heritage Center, University of Wyoming. The Irvin Department of Rare Books and Special Collections, University of South Carolina Library, granted access to the Rialto script. We thank the New York Public Library for the Performing Arts for copies of photographs from the 1926 production; Jeremy Megraw, Photograph Librarian at the Billy Rose Theatre Division, was especially helpful. We are grateful to Jade Broughton Adams and to Robert Trogdon, fellow Fitzgerald scholars, for sending materials to us.

Other than passing mention in standard biographies of Fitzgerald, the only commentary on the 1926 theatrical production is by David W. Cheatham, "Owen Davis's Dramatization of *The Great Gatsby*: A Comparative Study," M.A. thesis, Department of English, Colorado State University, Spring 1979.

NOTE ON THE TEXT

This edition presents the text of the Broadway script, preserved in the F. Scott Fitzgerald Additional Papers, Department of Rare Books and Manuscripts, Princeton University Library. No substantive emendations have been introduced. Obvious typographical errors have been silently corrected; a few marks of punctuation have been added for readability.

Studio portrait of Fitzgerald, taken in Nice, France, 1924.

INTRODUCTION

On Saturday evening, April 11, 1925, the theatrical impresario William A. Brady bought a copy of F. Scott Fitzgerald's new novel, *The Great Gatsby*, at a newsstand in Atlantic City, New Jersey. It was Easter weekend: Brady had spent that day watching tryouts for a production that he was mounting at Nixon's Apollo Theatre on New York Avenue, just off the Atlantic City Boardwalk. The copy of Fitzgerald's novel that he purchased must have been one of the first offered for sale. Charles Scribner's Sons had published the book the previous day, Friday, April 10. Brady began reading the novel that evening and was captured by the plot and characters. He read all night, finishing in the early hours of Sunday morning. He sensed that Fitzgerald's novel might be adapted for the Broadway stage. As soon as the telegraph office in Atlantic City opened on Monday, April 13, he wired his New York office with instructions to make an offer for dramatic rights.[1]

Brady, who was then sixty-one, was a veteran Broadway producer. He was involved in the movie business and was also a successful boxing promoter. As a boy he had sold newspapers on the street corners of New York City. At fifteen years of age he

[1] "Mr. Brady's Sleepless Night Put 'The Great Gatsby' on the Stage." Unattributed clipping in Scrapbook IV, F. Scott Fitzgerald Additional Papers, Princeton University Library. The scrapbook is unpaginated. Clippings and other materials that concern the stage production of *The Great Gatsby* are on inferential pages [78–106]. They are followed by photographs and clippings about the movie version. Images of the scrapbook are available on the website of the Department of Special Collections, Princeton University.

William A. Brady, Broadway producer and boxing promoter.

hitchhiked to San Francisco and became a bit-part player in small-time drama productions there. He learned the theater business, saved his money, and several years later returned to New York, where he began producing plays — some 260 by the end of his career. On the side he managed prizefighters, including two heavy-weight champions, James J. Jeffries and James J. "Gentleman Jim"

Corbett. He was a promoter and a hustler, with good instincts
about what might please the ticket-buying public.

To produce a script for the stage version, Brady secured the services of Owen Davis, then one of the most successful playwrights
on the New York scene. Three years earlier Davis had won the
Pulitzer Prize for his play *Icebound*, a family drama involving a
will, a surprise inheritance, and an unexpected romance.[2] Davis,
fifty-one years old, had earned a degree from Harvard but had
been an indifferent student there, more interested in athletics (he
was a sprinter and a football player) than in academic study. He
had begun a career in journalism by writing sketches about the
Tenderloin district of New York for the *Police Gazette*, a weekly
tabloid that specialized in crime, sports, celebrity gossip, and girlie
pin-ups. Davis wrote for the *Gazette* under several pseudonyms,
including Ike Swift, Martin Hurley, and Robert Wayne. Later he
served a long apprenticeship writing melodramas for the popular
theater circuit. Among his successful efforts were *Nellie, the Beautiful Cloak Model* (1906), *Chinatown Charlie* (1906), and *Dead-
wood Dick's Last Shot* (1907). By the mid-1920s he had managed
to have several of his plays presented on Broadway; by the end of
his career he had written or been involved in more than seventy
Broadway productions.[3]

[2] A movie version of the play, directed by William C. deMille (brother of the
director Cecil B. deMille), was released in 1924. The play was revived in the fall
of 2014 in a production at the Metropolitan Playhouse in New York City. See
Anita Gates, "The Weather Is Cold, the Feelings More So," *The New York Times*,
September 26, 2014, section C, p. 2.

[3] Fitzgerald, who was living in Paris, was pleased that Brady and Davis would
do the play. He wrote (ca. June 1, 1925) to Maxwell Perkins, his editor at Charles
Scribner's Sons: "Word has just come by cable that Brady has made an offer for
the dramatic rights of <u>Gatsby</u>, with Owen Davis, king of proffessional play doc-
tors, to do the dramatization. I am, needless to say, accepting, but please keep it
confidential until the actual contract is signed." *F. Scott Fitzgerald: A Life in Letters*, ed. Matthew J. Bruccoli (New York: Scribner, 1994): 117. Fitzgerald's errors
in spelling are preserved here and elsewhere.

Owen Davis, who adapted *The Great Gatsby* for the Broadway stage.

The Great Gatsby was one of Davis's first attempts to adapt a novel for the stage.[4] He found the process to be constricting.

[4] Six years later, in 1932, he and his son Donald Davis transformed Pearl S. Buck's *The Good Earth* into a long-running Broadway play; three years after that they turned Edith Wharton's novella *Ethan Frome* into a successful Broadway drama.

"It is, for me at any rate, far more difficult to make a play from some other person's novel than it is to build one out of my own fancy," he wrote in *The New York Times*. "Instead of being a never-failing adventure, it is simply a weary grind." He was envious of the brilliance of Fitzgerald's writing: "I couldn't for the life of me see why this boy, half my age, should be able to write a better yarn than I could possibly write." Davis felt, however, that he had done a reasonably good job of adapting Fitzgerald's novel. "It really would take a very clever man to make a bad play out of 'The Great Gatsby,'" he concluded.[5]

To direct the production Brady hired George Cukor, who was then only twenty-six years old. Cukor had started his career as a stage manager and bit-part actor. He began directing plays on the New York summer-stock circuit in 1920. His first Broadway drama, *Antonia*, opened at the Empire Theatre on October 20, 1925, and ran through December of that year. *The Great Gatsby* was his second Broadway production. Two years later he moved to Hollywood, where he became a successful film director. He is remembered today for such films as *Little Women* (1933), *The Philadelphia Story* (1940), and *My Fair Lady* (1964), for which he won the Academy Award for Best Director.

To play the part of Jay Gatsby, Brady secured the services of James Rennie, a popular leading man who was then appearing in both silent movies and in stage plays. After *The Great Gatsby* had finished its run, Rennie would make a successful transition to the "talkies" and star in several films, including *Girl of the Golden West* (1930), *Illicit* (1931), and *The Divorce Racket* (1932). In the mid-1930s he returned to the stage and appeared on Broadway and in touring productions into the late 1950s.[6]

[5] Owen Davis, "Making a Play from a Novel," *The New York Times*, March 28, 1926, p. X4. Portions of this article were reprinted in "Dramatizing Novel 'No Fun,'" *The Baltimore Sun*, October 17, 1926, p. 50.

[6] Fitzgerald wrote to Rennie ca. July 17, 1926, about an idea that Rennie had asked him to transform into a drama script. After initial efforts Fitzgerald declined

James Rennie played Jay Gatsby in the production.

Florence Eldridge, a rising star with aristocratic good looks, was signed to play Daisy Buchanan. Eldridge had begun her career as a chorus girl at the Astor Theatre in 1918. By the mid-1920s she, like Rennie, was appearing in both stage productions and silent films. In 1927 she married the actor Fredric March and, in the years that followed, played opposite him in many touring productions. Among the Broadway dramas in which she appeared were *The Skin of Our Teeth* (1942), *An Enemy of the People* (1950), and *Long Day's Journey into Night* (1956), for which she received a Tony nomination.[7]

The rest of the cast had a considerable amount of theatrical experience. Margherita Sargent, who took the role of Daisy's mother, had been appearing on Broadway since 1916 and would act in productions there until 1957. Edward H. Wever, who played Nick, was a Princeton alumnus who had been president of the Triangle Club (the student dramatic society) in his senior year; he appeared in thirteen Broadway productions between 1921 and 1929. Tom was played by Elliot Cabot, a member of the Cabot family of Boston; he had been educated at Harvard and at Caius College, Cambridge; he would appear on Broadway throughout

to pursue the project further. "I'm convinced that I'd simply ruin your idea," wrote Fitzgerald. The letter is published in *Correspondence of F. Scott Fitzgerald*, ed. Matthew J. Bruccoli and Margaret M. Duggan (New York: Random House, 1980): 197–8.

[7] On April 1, Eldridge was replaced in the production by Betty Wales, a lesser-known performer. "Florence Eldridge Ousted as 'The Great Gatsby' Star; Calls Brady's Action Funny," *Brooklyn Daily Eagle*, April 1, 1926, p. 12. In May, Eldridge (perhaps still under the spell of Fitzgerald's novel) purchased a three-quarter-acre plot in Great Neck at a new residential colony, called Kenilworth, in the King's Point section. According to the newspaper announcement of the purchase, the site "has an extensive view of Manhasset Bay and Long Island Sound. Miss Eldridge plans to build a home there which she will occupy herself." "Actress Buys Home Site," *Brooklyn Times-Union*, May 15, 1926, p. 9.

Florence Eldridge took the part of Daisy Buchanan.

the remainder of the 1920s and into the early 1930s. Charles Dickson, who was signed for the role of Wolfshiem, was a veteran actor who had been appearing on Broadway since 1887. Catherine Willard, as Jordan, was in her third Broadway play and would go on to appear in productions into the early 1950s. Porter Hall, as Doc Civet, stayed busy on Broadway through the 1920s; in 1931 he went to Hollywood and became a character actor. He appeared in numerous movies, including *The Thin Man* (1934), *Mr. Smith Goes to Washington* (1939), *Double Indemnity* (1944), and *Miracle on 34th Street* (1947).

Virginia Hennings took the role of the "colored maid" Sally, a part added by Davis. She must have played the part in blackface. *The Great Gatsby* was her only recorded appearance on Broadway. She had been in vaudeville productions in Philadelphia since at least 1909 (often listed as a "character impersonator"), and by 1916 she was appearing in silent movies. A photograph published in *The Philadelphia Inquirer* in December 1917 reveals that she was white.[8] Hennings later formed her own company and appeared on stage in Philadelphia and in road productions in New Jersey and Washington, DC. African Americans had been appearing in all-Black productions on Broadway since the late 1890s, but the first production with a racially integrated cast was *Show Boat*, which opened in December 1927, almost two years after *The Great Gatsby* began its run. Having a cast member perform in blackface in *The Great Gatsby* would not have raised eyebrows at the time.

An early version of Owen Davis's script was sent to Fitzgerald, who was in Switzerland with his wife, Zelda, and their daughter Scottie. In a letter sent ca. January 19, 1926, Fitzgerald wrote to Max Perkins, expressing misgivings about how much of Nick's elevated language had been used as dialogue in the script. Perkins attended a pre-Broadway performance in Stamford, Connecticut,

---

[8] "She's a 'Glad' Girl," *The Philadelphia Inquirer*, December 9, 1917, p. 42.

Charles Dickson, a Broadway veteran, played Meyer Wolfshiem.

on Wednesday, January 27, and on the next day wrote a reassuring letter to Fitzgerald:

You need not feel ashamed of the play.... Your ideas and the course of the action have been adhered to far more closely than I ever dreamed they would be. The cast is excellent, especially Gatsby, Buchanan, Daisy, and Wolfshiem.... And all the individuals I saw, like the Burts who went with me, and Bob Benchley, who was in the lobby after the second act, were much pleased.... "The Great Gatsby" is distinctly well done. It is certainly a good play, and highly interesting, and it seems to me it has an excellent chance for success.[9]

During the last week of January, *The Great Gatsby* had a second out-of-town opening on Long Island, at the Great Neck Playhouse — this to iron out the kinks and get the show ready for Broadway. The production opened to a full house on Tuesday, February 2, 1926, at the Ambassador Theatre, 219 West 49th Street, between Broadway and Eighth Avenue.[10] In the audience that night were Mr. and Mrs. Charles Scribner; Mr. and Mrs. Harold Ober; the producers Jesse L. Lasky, Samuel Goldwyn, Gilbert Miller, and Jules Brulatour; the actors Henry Clapp Smith, Margaret Illington,

---

[9] *Dear Scott/Dear Max*, ed. John Kuehl and Jackson Bryer (New York: Scribner, 1971): 131. "Burt" is Maxwell Struthers Burt, a Scribner author. "Bob Benchley" is Robert Benchley, the humorist, newspaper columnist, and member of the Algonquin Round Table.

[10] The theatre, which still stands, was then relatively new. It had been built in 1921 by the Shubert Brothers, theatrical managers and producers, as one of four theatres they erected in New York during the post-World War I period. The Ambassador is an unusual performance space. It was built at a diagonal on its site so that the maximum number of seats could be created. The auditorium, elaborately decorated, is hexagonal in shape, with a relatively small proscenium and limited room in the stage wings. Despite these oddities the Ambassador has proved to be a popular venue. Among the productions there over the years have been *The Lion in Winter* (1966), *Godspell* (1977), *A View from the Bridge* (1983), *Bring in 'da Noise, Bring in 'da Funk* (1996), and, in revival, *Chicago* (2003).

Interior of the Ambassador Theatre, where *The Great Gatsby*
had its premiere.

Alice Brady, and Hope Hampton; the radio personality Major
Edward Bowes; and other New York celebrities and luminaries.[11]
The next morning Charles Scribner sent a telegram to Fitzgerald
at the Hotel Bellevue, Salies de Béarn, in the French Pyrenees:
"GATSBY GREAT SUCCESS ... REVIEWS EXCELLENT." Ober
also sent a wire: "AUDIENCE ENTHUSIASTIC OVER GATSBY.
PLAY CARRIED GLAMOR OF STORY. EXCELLENTLY CAST
AND ACTED. REVIEWS ALL VERY FAVORABLE." An unidenti-
fied friend sent a shorter telegram: "GOOD PLAY. SHOULD COIN
MONEY."[12]

Reviews of the play were favorable. J. Brooks Atkinson, in *The
New York Times*, showed some familiarity with Fitzgerald's novel.
The production "retains most of the novel's peculiar glamour,"
he wrote. "By use of people in the flesh, speaking and acting, the
play accents the telling contrasts between Gatsby, the romantic
swindler, positive and honorable according to his precedents, and
the Buchanans and Bakers and people of quality who have a high
sense of honor and cheat it continually."[13] Alexander Woollcott, in
the *World*, wrote that Davis had "carried the book over on to the
stage with almost the minimum of spillage," and that the cast had
been "goaded into giving a vociferous performance." In the *Sun*,
Gilbert Gabriel wrote: "More entertaining drama has not come
out of a book in a long time." Frank Vreeland, in the *Evening Telegram*, called the production "one of the very best that Owen Davis
ever tossed off between rounds of golf." E. W. Osborne, the critic
for the *Evening World*, praised the performances of individual actors: James Rennie was "almost ideally fitted in every particular
to the Gatsby role"; Florence Eldridge, as Daisy, was "delightfully

[11] "Bootless Bootlegging," *The New York Evening Telegram*, Scrapbook IV.
[12] These telegrams were preserved by Fitzgerald in Scrapbook IV. The telegram
from Ober is published in *As Ever, Scott Fitz—*, ed. Matthew J. Bruccoli and
Jennifer McCabe Atkinson (Philadelphia and New York: Lippincott, 1972): 85.
[13] "Careless People and Gatsby," *The New York Times*, February 3, 1926, p. 22.

full of life"; Catherine Willard was "a blooming and charming Jordan Baker." Percy Hammond in the *Herald-Tribune* singled out Owen Davis for the adaptation: "Mr. Davis's dramatization was so able that it managed to emphasize the subtle qualities of Mr. Fitzgerald's study of a golden vagabond without causing the usual epidemic of gooseflesh."[14]

We should not be surprised by the reception: The Broadway production of *The Great Gatsby* is an entertaining play about the idle rich, with jazz music, wild parties, and bootlegging. Some of the characters are wealthy, but others are from the underclass, and still others are criminals and gangsters. Prohibition was in effect in 1926, but almost everyone in the play has a drink in hand. The women have bobbed hair, wear short skirts, and smoke cigarettes. Everyone knows the latest dance steps. The plot involves adultery, deception, revenge, and murder. Davis managed to extract these elements and fashion them into a fast-moving drama.

Fitzgerald read these notices, and a good many others, while he was in Europe. Ober sent over the opening-night reviews. Fitzgerald subscribed to a clipping service, had the subsequent publicity mailed to him, and pasted everything into a scrapbook he was compiling for *The Great Gatsby*. Some of these reviews and articles are difficult to trace now because the headlines, by-lines, and other publication data have been snipped off. Fortunately, images of the pages from the scrapbook are available on the website of the Special Collections Department at Princeton University Library. The reviews and other publicity, all of it in Scrapbook IV, can be seen on the Special Collections website.

In February 1926, when *The Great Gatsby* opened, Broadway was flourishing. New theaters were being erected, and attendance was high. The post-World War I economic boom had made live theater popular and profitable. Competition for the entertainment dollar was stiff: on opening night for *The Great Gatsby* there were

[14] These clippings, all from February 2, are preserved in Scrapbook IV.

A caricature of James Rennie.

more than one hundred choices for an evening's distraction in the city — dramas, musicals, concerts, stage shows, and movies. Devotees of serious drama could see Henrik Ibsen's *Hedda Gabler*, G. B. Shaw's *Arms and the Man*, or Eugene O'Neill's *The Great God Brown*. Music fans could hear the New York Symphony, the

Boston Symphony, or "1,200 Male Voices" in a concert presented by the Associated Glee Clubs. Movies showing in the Broadway cinema palaces were General Lew Wallace's *Ben-Hur* (the Fitzgeralds had visited the set for this movie while it was being filmed in Rome) and *Stella Dallas*, starring the young actress Lois Moran, whom Fitzgerald would later use as the model for Rosemary Hoyt in *Tender Is the Night*. If one wanted a comedy, the choices included *Is Zat So?* at the Central, *Laff That Off* at Wallack's, *Puppy Love* at the 48th Street Theater, and *Easy Come Easy Go* at the Biltmore. Leggy variety shows were *Artists and Models (Paris Edition)*, *Gay Paree*, George White's *Scandals*, and Earl Carroll's *Vanities*. Among the long-running productions were *No, No, Nanette!* at the Globe and *Abie's Irish Rose* at the Republic. Some of the stage and screen stars appearing that night were Norma Shearer, Ina Claire, George Jessel, Peggy Hopkins Joyce, John Barrymore, Lon Chaney, Marilyn Miller, and the Marx Brothers.[15]

From mid-June 1925 to mid-June 1926, some 262 productions were mounted on Broadway. There were 171 dramas, twenty-four musicals, eighteen revues, thirty revivals, fifteen return engagements, two "foreign presentations," and two "miscellaneous" shows. Long-running productions were *Cradle Snatchers*, at 338 performances, and *The Jazz Singer*, at 309 performances. *The Butter and Egg Man* made it to 243 performances; *Love 'Em and Leave 'Em* lasted for 158; *Naughty Cinderella* reached 121. *The Great Gatsby* had a respectable run of 112 performances, counting matinées — good enough for twenty-eighth place among the dramas in 1926. (A stage version of *The Green Hat*, by Fitzgerald's fellow novelist and competitor Michael Arlen, scored 237 performances and occupied ninth place on the list.) Many of the dramas made it to fifty performances. Flops included *So That's*

---

[15] Display ads, *New York Times*, February 2, 1926, p. 21.

That, *You Can't Win*, and *Dope*, each with two performances, and *Beyond Evil*, which opened and closed on the same night.[16]

The New York production of *The Great Gatsby* was scheduled to end in the first week of May, but ticket sales were strong enough for its run to be extended to May 22. The play then moved to Chicago, with the opening planned for August 1, the first night of the theatre season there. Brady took some of the cast of the New York production to Chicago. James Rennie continued as Gatsby, Catherine Willard as Jordan, and Charles Dickson as Wolfshiem. Other roles were filled by replacements: Helen Baxter appeared as Daisy, Walter Davis as Tom, and Monroe Owsley as Nick. Elsa Gray, who later became one of the original New York Roxy Girls, played the role of Sally.

The cast began rehearsals in the Studebaker Theatre, an ornate auditorium on South Michigan Avenue, built in 1898 and expanded in the early 1920s. There a serious mishap occurred. On July 31, the day before the play was to open, Brady was rehearsing the cast on the Studebaker stage when he tripped and fell into the orchestra pit. He was carried unconscious to his hotel room; the house physician announced to the press later that Brady had broken his wrist. The rehearsal continued, however, and the play opened on schedule the following night.[17]

Notices were good. The anonymous reviewer for the *Chicago Tribune* praised the performances of James Rennie and Catherine Willard: "If you've read the novel, you'll like the play." Amy Leslie, reviewing in the *Chicago Daily News*, reported that there had been a "huge crowd" for opening night, and that "the audience seemed enthralled." She, too, praised Rennie ("he speaks the Michigan language of the Fitzgerald hero") and Willard (she

---

[16] "Facts and Figures of the Past Season," *The New York Times*, June 20, 1926, p. X1.

[17] "William A. Brady Injured in Fall," *The New York Times*, August 1, 1926, p. 30.

played Jordan Baker "with a captivating impudence and calm").[18] The play had been scheduled for a four-week run but was extended for another four weeks and had its final performance in late September. The production then traveled to the Shubert Theatre in New York for a one-week return engagement beginning October 4. With a different cast it moved on to Brooklyn, Baltimore, Philadelphia, Detroit, St. Louis, Denver, and possibly to other cities, each time for a one-week stand.[19] The last notice located for a road production was in Minneapolis, opening on January 30, 1927.[20]

In order to understand Davis's adaptation it helps to look at his memoir *I'd Like to Do It Again*, published in 1931, five years after *The Great Gatsby* opened on Broadway. In the book Davis reminisces about the years that he spent in regional theatre, manufacturing melodramas for the popular stage. "The good playmaker of the popular-priced theater was supposed to know what a proper list of characters for a play must be," Davis tells us. He always began with a cast of eight in mind: the Hero, the Heroine, the Heavy Man, the Heavy Woman, the Soubrette, the Comedian, the Light Comedy Boy, and the Second Heavy. "These eight made up the cast," he explains, "and to them we added two or three utility actors to play such 'walking parts' as the plot demanded, but no matter what the play these eight characters were always

---

[18] Scrapbook IV.

[19] Notices and advertisements: *Brooklyn Times Union*, October 12, 1926, p. 13; *The Baltimore Sun*, October 19, 1926, p. 13; *The Philadelphia Inquirer*, October 26, 1926, p. 14; *Minneapolis Star Tribune*, February 1, 1927, p. 13. Fitzgerald made note of the Detroit, St. Louis, and Denver productions in his ledger entry for 1926.

[20] "'The Great Gatsby' Is Drama Offered by Bainbridge Players," *Minneapolis Star Tribune*, January 30, 1927, p. 51.

in it." [21] It's not too much of a stretch to see the actors in Davis's adaptation of *The Great Gatsby* as filling these roles. He reveals another secret of the trade: "One of the first tricks I learned was that my plays must be written for an audience who, owing to the huge, uncarpeted, noisy theaters, wouldn't always hear the words and who, a large percentage of them having only recently landed in America, couldn't have understood them in any case." His solution: "I therefore wrote for the eye rather than the ear and played out each emotion in action" (pp. 36–37). Dialogue was secondary. The plays were driven by movement.

Davis took many liberties with Fitzgerald's storyline. He disassembled the novel, rearranged its parts into a prologue and three acts, and made the action chronological. Information about Jay Gatsby's past, revealed to us gradually in the novel, is now presented all at once, early in the script. Nick is no longer the narrator; he is only Gatsby's neighbor and friend. Lines from the novel have been extracted and put into the mouths of the actors. Lines spoken by one character in the novel, however, are often given to another character in the play. New characters have been invented — among them Daisy's mother, Mrs. Amy Fay; the "colored maid" Sally; an army major named Will Carson; an Irish butler named Ryan; and two criminals named Donnivan and Crosby. Nothing is said in the script about East versus West. Gatsby still uses the expression "old sport," but only a few times.

Many of Gatsby's lines, in the prologue and elsewhere in the script, are taken from the novel, where they are narrated in Nick's voice. In the prologue, for example, Gatsby says: "There seemed to be a stir and bustle among the stars. I could see, out of the corner of my eye, the blocks of the sidewalks in the moonlight and I had the fancy that they formed a ladder that mounted to a secret place above the trees...." And later: "For a moment, to listen just

---

[21] Davis, *I'd Like to Do It Again* (New York: Farrar and Rinehart, Inc., 1931): 101–5.

once more to the tuning fork I had struck upon a star, then — I kissed you, and as my lips touched yours you blossomed for me like a flower." There are no stage directions here, but almost certainly these lines (if they survived into performance) were meant to be delivered as soliloquies. Perhaps Gatsby stood in a spotlight and addressed the audience directly. Otherwise these set speeches would have seemed quite artificial.[22]

Much has been dispensed with. There is no opening luncheon at the Buchanan house, no trip through the Valley of Ashes, no party at Tom and Myrtle's love nest, and no scene at the Plaza Hotel. There is no billboard with the painted eyes of Doctor T. J. Eckleburg, nor is there a guest list for Gatsby's fabulous parties. Gatsby does not take Daisy on a tour of his mansion; Klipspringer does not play the piano or do his liver exercises; Gatsby does not display his shirts. Nick and Jordan are a couple, but their romance is not particularly important. Daisy's voice is no longer full of money; she seems interested only in a fling with Gatsby.

Wolfshiem still has cuff buttons made from human molars, still speaks in a Yiddish accent, and is still the man who fixed the 1919 World's Series. His character, however, has been altered. He has become a friendly fellow who drives out to Long Island to visit Gatsby at his estate, misses the turn-off, and ends up at Nick's cottage. Tom's interest in eugenics and racial purity has been downplayed. In this production Myrtle has become a former chorus girl, now married to the renamed "Buck" Wilson, an ex-prizefighter who has become a chauffeur. Owl Eyes is missing, not present in Gatsby's library nor anywhere else in the play. Gone are Gatsby's yellow car and his pink suit. The green light, thank goodness, is still visible across the bay.

---

[22] Fitzgerald seems to have written to Rennie, expressing his worries about overblown dialogue. Rennie wrote back to him in an undated letter, "I am certain you have one of the earlier scripts where 'Gatsby' is much more flowery than we are doing him now." Scrapbook IV.

Fitzgerald was in Europe when Davis was preparing the script and, later, when rehearsals were being held. Perhaps this was just as well; he must have felt proprietary about *The Great Gatsby*. If he had been allowed to attend rehearsals, he would undoubtedly have been a pain in the neck. In fact anyone who reads the script today will probably react as Fitzgerald would have. *The Great Gatsby* has become a secular scripture, a verbal icon. Many of us have read and taught the novel so often that we have it almost by heart. We should remember that, in 1926, *The Great Gatsby* was not yet a classic work of literature. It was a new novel by a popular young author. Reviews of the book had been largely positive; sales had been moderately strong. Davis's assignment was to transform Fitzgerald's story into a play that could be staged on Broadway. He needed familiar character types and a straightforward plot; he also needed action, humor, and romance. In his script he provided all of these elements and managed to transform the novel into an evening of first-rate entertainment.

Two versions of the Owen Davis script survive. Both are in typescript. The first of these, which we shall call the "Broadway script," is the earlier and longer of the two. A photocopy of this earlier text is at Princeton in the F. Scott Fitzgerald Additional Papers (Box 1b, Folder 15).[23] A photocopy of another typescript of this earlier version survives in the Bruccoli Collection at the University of South Carolina. Also in the Bruccoli Collection is an original carbon typescript of this same text, a page-by-page transcription of the dialogue and stage directions marked "Tom Buchanan" in

---

[23] The original of this copy seems to have belonged to George Cukor, who directed the Broadway production. The copy is marked with directions for the actors, indicating where they should begin a scene and where they should move in the action that follows.

pencil on the cover.[24] And a third exemplar of this earlier and
longer version survives in a collection of Owen Davis scripts at
the American Heritage Center, University of Wyoming. The fact
that all three of these early versions are page-by-page transcripts
(but not line-by-line) suggests that they were prepared for actors,
directors, and others involved in the Broadway production. During rehearsals and script conferences, everyone would have needed to be quite literally "on the same page."

The second and shorter version of the script survives in only one
copy known to us. This copy is in the Bruccoli Collection at the
University of South Carolina. It is the original of a mimeographed
script, bound in heavy paper covers and secured with brass fasteners. This script was produced at the Rialto Service Bureau, a
mimeographing and typing agency then located (according to the
printing on the cover of this script) at 229 West 42nd Street in
New York. This "Rialto script" includes sketches of the sets, handdrawn onto the stencils, and two pages of lighting directions. In
the Rialto version, a good many changes have been made. The
prologue has been cut from fifteen typed pages to ten and has
been moved from the living room of Daisy's house to the front
porch. The dialogue has been trimmed and tightened. The remainder of the text (the three acts that constitute the body of the play)
has been revised and polished, with occasional cutting to the text
in order to move the action along.

For this edition we are reproducing the text of Broadway script,
which we believe to be the earlier and more authoritative of the
two versions.[25] The Broadway text shows more clearly the process

[24] This might be the copy used by Elliot Cabot, who played Tom on Broadway.
Three pages in this copy are deleted with black X-marks. The provenance of this
copy is unknown.

[25] The Broadway script is paginated from P–1 to P–15 for the prologue; from
1–1 to 1–30 for Act I, from 2–1 to 2–28 for Act II, and from 3–1 to 3–27 for Act
III.

by which Owen Davis adapted Fitzgerald's novel for the stage. But the play seen on Broadway, or on the road, might well have been different from either of the surviving scripts. Changes in dialogue and action are frequently made in rehearsals and even during the run of a play. It is impossible to know how much was conveyed by voice and gesture, staging and lighting, costumes and makeup, sets and props, movement and music. Everything in a novel is done with words and by the imagination of the reader. Everything in a play is a collaboration. The participants are the dramatist, the actors, the director, the musicians, the makeup artists, the costume designers, the dressers, the lighting technicians, the stagehands, and the audience members. When a novel is published, it is fixed in paper and ink. So long as a single copy survives, the text survives. Once a play is performed, by contrast, that performance vanishes. The play can only be brought back to life in the next performance.

One thing is certain: the audience got its money's worth. So did Fitzgerald. During the New York run, box seats went for $3.20, orchestra seats for $3.00, gallery for $2.50, and balcony for $1.00. Four of the clippings in Fitzgerald's scrapbook, all of them headed "Box Office Takings," provide approximate figures about ticket sales and attendance. In one of its best weeks the play took in $16,000, in another week $15,500, in a third $14,000, and in a fourth $11,500. The top earners during these same weeks were *A Night in Paris* with an average gross of $20,500, *Artists and Models* averaging $21,000, and *The Cocoanuts* (the musical, with the Marx Brothers) averaging $24,000. Among the dramas, *The Great Gatsby* was ahead of *Twelve Miles Out*, another play about a bootlegger, which was averaging $10,500, but a bit behind *The Green Hat*, which was taking in $16,500.

The contract for drama rights was structured so that Fitzgerald's earnings were calculated on percentages of the weekly box office. He received 40 percent of 5 percent of the first $5,000. Then his share went up to 40 percent of 7.5 percent of the next $2,000, and forty percent of 10 percent of everything over $7,000.[26] Fitzgerald did well by this contract. He recorded his payments on the pages of his business ledger for 1925 and 1926. He received $1,000 as an advance; then he was paid $2,907 from the New York run, $2,971 from the Chicago production, and $751 from road performances. His total earnings were $7,629, on which he paid a 10 percent commission to Ober. It is difficult to calculate the value of the dollar across time, but in today's money, almost one hundred years after the play opened, the buying power of the payments to Fitzgerald comes to almost $103,000. He did not have to lift a finger to collect the money; it came to him as a bonus for having created the novel.

Fitzgerald never saw a performance of the Owen Davis play. Surely he was happy about its success, but he must have regretted not having been there for the New York opening or the production in Chicago. He would have enjoyed the New York production and the performances in Chicago and Minneapolis (adjacent to St. Paul, his home town). He might have taken a bow at the final curtain on opening night on Broadway. He and Zelda might have been given walk-on parts for a few performances in New York or on the road. He would certainly have been interviewed by reporters; he and Zelda would have had their pictures taken for the Sunday newspapers.

[26] For details of the contract see *As Ever*, 79n. In a letter to Harold Ober written in late May 1926, Fitzgerald estimates that the play "put in my pocket seventeen or eighteen thousand without a stroke of work on my part" (*As Ever*, 91). Evidence of income from the play in these amounts is not present in the Ledger. Possibly Fitzgerald was counting other recent income, including money for the movie rights, in his estimate.

The Great Gatsby appeared on Broadway at the right moment. Thousands of people saw the production in New York, or in Chicago, or another city. The play made Fitzgerald a substantial amount of money and spread his name across the country. During all of this activity, alas, he was biding his time in Salies-de-Béarn, a village in the Swiss Pyrenees famous for its salt baths. Zelda was taking a cure for colitis. It was the off-season there, and nothing much was happening. "We are two of seven guests in the only open hotel," he reported to Ober in a letter.[27] In the meantime "The Rich Boy" was appearing in *Red Book* (in two parts, January and February 1926). *All the Sad Young Men*, Fitzgerald's third collection of short fiction, was published to favorable reviews on February 26. The volume, which included several of Fitzgerald's best stories, would sell 16,000 copies, an excellent performance for a book of short fiction. Fitzgerald's name was everywhere. He was at the peak of his powers as a writer and at the height of his fame as a literary celebrity. How could he have imagined that it would all someday end?

By September 1939, matters had changed considerably for Fitzgerald, for publishers, for Broadway, for America and the world. The "war to end wars," the Great War in which Fitzgerald (along with his characters Nick Carraway and Jay Gatsby) had served, had not in fact ended war. After a seizure of power beginning in 1933, Adolf Hitler sent the German army into Poland on September 1. France and Britain declared war on Germany two days later.

Fitzgerald was living in Encino, California. He was in poor health and out of a job after several contract stints with Metro-Goldwyn-Mayer as a screenwriter. He had been working

---

[27] *As Ever*, 84. The letter, undated, arrived at Ober's offices on February 4, 1926, two days after the play had opened.

in Hollywood since the summer of 1937, but with little success. Zelda was in treatment at the Highland Hospital in Asheville, North Carolina, and Scottie was at Vassar College. Fitzgerald was paying the bills at both institutions. When he least expected it and most needed it, Owen Davis's play of *The Great Gatsby* did him a surprise favor.

On September 19, 1939, Fitzgerald wrote to Harold Ober of his current situation: "Very encouraging. Almost as much fun as the war. I've had two picture offers since I began to walk again last July. Each for one week. The last one paid the income tax and left a cash balance of $38.00 .... I can't keep Scottie in school." Ober replied with a telegram: "HAVE OFFER ONE MORNING BROAD-CAST OF GREAT GATSBY YOUR SHARE $250 OWEN DAVIS ARRANGING THIS WITH HIS PLAY ETHAN FROME SHALL I ACCEPT." Fitzgerald wired back immediately: "ALL RIGHT WITH ME ABOUT GATSBY PLEASE AIR MAIL ME WHEN AND WHAT STATION." Fitzgerald then sent a second telegram to Ober: "IF YOU CAN SEND HALF THAT MONEY TO THE COMPTROLLER AT VASSAR IT WOULD HELP." Although the money from the radio broadcast of the play would not arrive for some months, Ober sent the $125 to Vassar right away.[28]

This must have been heartening to Fitzgerald, who had been disappointed a year before when Davis turned down the chance to make a drama of *Tender Is the Night* (1934). Fitzgerald had hoped for the novel to become a hit play or movie, or both. By the autumn of 1936, however, Davis had turned down the invitation to adapt *Tender Is the Night* for the stage. Fitzgerald wrote to Perkins: "I know that Davis who had every reason to undertake it after the success of Gatsby simply turned thumbs down from his dramatist's instinct that the story was not constructed as dramatically as Gatsby and did not readily lend itself to dramatization."[29]

[28] *As Ever*, 414–15.
[29] Fitzgerald to Perkins, October 16, 1936. *Dear Scott/Dear Max*, 233.

Davis regularly had versions of his plays broadcast as radio adaptations in the late 1930s. He and his son Donald, who was by the
mid-1930s collaborating with Davis, wrote the script for *Ethan
Frome* from Edith Wharton's 1911 novel after Wharton herself
suggested Davis.[30] The play, starring Pauline Lord, with Ruth
Gordon and Raymond Massey as the doomed lovers, opened on
Broadway in January 1936 at the National Theatre on 41st Street
to excellent reviews. The play script was published in an attractive
clothbound edition by Scribner's in the same month.

   When Davis was approached for those radio dramatizations in
the autumn of 1939, *Ethan Frome*, which had revitalized his own
career, and *The Great Gatsby* — both based on tragic love stories by prominent American novelists — were the plays he chose.
Davis's inclusion of *Gatsby* helped Fitzgerald at a low point, providing enough money to pay Scottie's college semester costs and
to cover other bills for the next months of 1939, until a $250
payment from *Esquire* for the short story "Pat Hobby's Christmas
Wish" marked, for Fitzgerald, a new source of income and the
start of a series of increasingly highly regarded short stories, the
last he would write.

[30] *Newsweek*, February 1, 1936: 33.

THE

GREAT
GATSBY

BY

OWEN DAVIS

BASED UPON THE NOVEL BY

F. SCOTT FITZGERALD

CHARACTERS

IN THE PROLOGUE

Major Carson   Sally
Mrs. Fay   Lieutenant Jay Gatsby
Daisy   Captain Buchanan

IN THE PLAY

Gatsby   Wilson
Nick Carraway   Daisy Buchanan
Tom Buchanan   Jordan Baker
Meyer Wolfshiem   Myrtle Wilson
Ryan

AT GATSBY'S

Doc Civet   Maud Turner
Milton Gay   Donnivan
Tom Turner   Crosby
Mrs. Gay

SCENES

PROLOGUE

September 1917 — the Fays' sitting room
in Louisville, Kentucky

ACT I

August 1925 — Nick Carraway's cottage at West Egg, L.I.

ACT II

Gatsby's library — one week later

ACT III

The same — ten days after

PROLOGUE

SCENE

The Fays' living room in Louisville,
Kentucky in September 1917.

Mrs. Fay, a well-dressed woman of middle age, stands by the open French windows at left, and looks anxiously out toward the garden. It is war time and in the distance a military band is playing "Over There." It is an old-fashioned Southern room, stately and elegant, but the set should be shallow so that a quick change, not over two minutes, may be made to the next scene. There is a door to hall at right. Mrs. Fay evidently hears some one coming for she stops to open window and calls.

MRS. FAY: Sally! Is that you?

(Sally, a middle aged colored servant, enters from veranda)

SALLY: Yes, yes Miss Amy, dat am me.

MRS. FAY: Was she there? Answer me! Can't you find her, Sally?

SALLY: Now Miss Amy child, don't you get all excited!

MRS. FAY *(impatiently)*: Sally! Was she there or wasn't she?

SALLY: Well — she wasn't exactly there.

MRS. FAY: How long had she been gone?

SALLY: Quite some time.

MRS. FAY *(sternly)*:   How long?

SALLY: Well of course if a person has got to be absolutely truth telling exact about it she ain't been there at all.

MRS. FAY *(sternly)*:   Then she told me a deliberate falsehood!

SALLY: You talk wicked and foolish Miss Amy! Dat ain't no falsehood — Jes' fo' a young lady of quality to tell her Ma dat she is where she ain't!

MRS. FAY *(distressed)*:   She lied to me!

SALLY: Go along with you! You didn't call it no lie when you used to do it to your Ma!

MRS. FAY: Is she with this young Lieutenant from Camp Taylor?

SALLY: I don't know no more about where dat child is dan you does.

MRS. FAY: Run out to the garage and see if her runabout is there!

SALLY *(reluctantly)*:   Well, it ain't exactly there Miss Amy.

MRS. FAY: You mean it's gone! She's out with this young Gatsby again!

SALLY *(with ready loyalty)*:   Dey ain't nobody ever born as fine a young lady as Miss Daisy is! You wasn't no finer yourself! You was mighty fine, but you wasn't no finer!

MRS. FAY: Be quiet!

SALLY: Yes ma'am. He's got a uniform, ain't he? He's goin' to fight the Germans, ain't he?

MRS. FAY: I wish he'd hurry up and do it! There isn't a mother in Louisville who has had an hour's peace since they opened Camp Taylor!

(A bell rings outside)

See who that is Sally!

(She is startled by the bell)

SALLY: Now don't you get scared! Miss Daisy is all right.

MRS. FAY: Go to the door!

SALLY: Yes, Miss Amy.

(She exits. Mrs. Fay crosses to French windows and looks out anxiously. Sally re-enters with Major Carson, a middle aged officer in a service uniform)

SALLY: Hit's Major Carson!

MRS. FAY: This is good of you, Will.

MAJOR: How are you, Amy?

(He takes her hand)

Thanks, Sally.

SALLY: Thank you, Major.

(She exits)

MRS. FAY: I am anxious, Will!

MAJOR: What's the trouble? Still this young Gatsby?

MRS. FAY: Daisy is out with him again! And only last night I scolded her for coming home so late.

MAJOR: Oh well. A wartime flirtation! All the girls are doing it.

MRS. FAY: But they are not all doing it with men like this! I am afraid of him, Will. He's absurd, but he is dangerous. He is as romantic as a gypsy, handsome, arrogant, ambitious — I have never seen such pride and I don't know where he gets it, or what right he has to any pride at all! Of course it is silly of me — Daisy couldn't really be serious about him!

MAJOR: I hope not.

(He takes a paper from his pocket)

Here is his record. The Intelligence Department took their time about it, but it is fairly complete.

MRS. FAY: Of course he isn't anybody! I don't have to ask you to have him looked up to be sure of that.

MAJOR: No, he isn't anybody, unless having the makings in him of becoming a good soldier counts.

MRS. FAY: It doesn't count! Not when it's Daisy's future.

MAJOR: I suppose not.

(He holds up the paper he has taken from his pocket)

"James Gatz" this boy's name seems really, or at least legally, to be Gatz, not Gatsby. He was and is nobody in particular. Five years ago he was a kid around the water front on Lake Superior, a clam digger, salmon fisher, any sort of job that would get him a bed and enough to eat.

MRS. FAY *(dismayed)*: It's the war! It's the uniform! Our girls never knew such people!

MAJOR: The boy has spirit, plenty of it, and a belief in himself and his future that is almost fantastic. In some way he was able to catch the attention of an eccentric yacht owner, Dan Cody, and was taken on board.

MRS. FAY: John used to speak of Dan Cody, the Nevada millionaire.

MAJOR: Yes — this boy, now calling himself Jay Gatsby, remained with Cody for three years. He was a steward, mate, skipper, secretary, and even jailor, for Dan Cody trusted him and grew to depend on him — they lived on the yacht for three years — until Cody died of drink — died a bankrupt as it turned out — then the war came along and Gatsby came here to Camp Taylor from his training camp.

MRS. FAY *(nervously)*: And Daisy is out somewhere with him! With a man like that!

MAJOR: It's all right, Amy.

MRS. FAY: No! Tom Buchanan is in town! His regiment sails from New York next week and he came all the way to say goodbye to her!

MAJOR: Young Buchanan! I see.

MRS. FAY: It isn't only because he has money. He has literally everything that a girl like Daisy cares for!

MAJOR: Yes.

MRS. FAY: And she really likes him, Will, this other thing is just a silly girl's excitement over the uniform.

MAJOR: Gatsby needn't trouble you after tonight, Amy, his regiment leaves tomorrow.

MRS. FAY *(startled)*:   For France!

MAJOR: Overseas — so unless she really cares for him —

MRS. FAY: Of course she doesn't!

MAJOR: Then that's the end of poor Gatsby!

(Sally enters)

SALLY: Mr. Tom Buchanan done came! He certainly does look big and fine in his uniform. Shall I fetch him in here, Miss Amy, or shall I sit him in the drawin' room?

MRS. FAY *(to Major)*:   I hoped he'd keep away until tomorrow! I really don't know what to say to him. You must help me, Will.

MAJOR: Between us we can hold the fort until Daisy gets back.

MRS. FAY: Put some of these lights out and lock the windows, Sally. It's after eleven o'clock.

(Mrs. Fay and Major exit to the hall. Sally throws out the electric side lights leaving a table lamp and a flood of moonlight from the open French windows. Sally is about to

cross to shut the windows when there is a low laugh outside in a girl's voice. Sally stops, a little startled, as Daisy Fay comes from the veranda. Daisy wears an evening gown of the fashion of 1917; she is a slight young girl, eager and excited)

DAISY: Hello!

(As she sees Sally)

Oh, it's you, Sally! Hush.

(She turns and speaks over her shoulder)

It's all right, Lieutenant Gatsby!

(Gatsby enters)

GATSBY: Well, Sally!

SALLY *(in low tone)*: Her Ma's in there an' she's awful mad 'bout you all bein' out so late without her knowin' where you all was.

GATSBY: It's the last time, Sally, she needn't grudge me that.

DAISY: He's going in the morning, Sally. I don't know what I am going to do!

SALLY: Not going to de war!

GATSBY: Yes.

DAISY: Tomorrow!

(She sobs and sits in chair at L.)

SALLY: Now baby!

(She crosses toward her)

GATSBY: Run along, Sally, don't tell anyone that we are here. I want to say goodbye. I won't keep her but a minute.

SALLY: Dey is company for her, an' her Ma is mighty mad!

GATSBY: She ought to be grateful, Sally, tell her so in the morning. Tell her I left for France, as a personal favor to her, and to a few others.

DAISY *(who is crying)*: Please do, Sally.

SALLY: I'll try, but yo' Ma is an awful noticing kind, Miss Daisy.

(She exits)

DAISY *(to Gatsby)*: I'm a fool to cry! I've never been so silly. I don't know why I am crying — Oh, I have never been so unhappy.

GATSBY: And I've never been so happy.

DAISY: It's awful to be the one to stay at home!

GATSBY: Of course it is.

DAISY: I hate the war!

GATSBY: It gives me the chance I need. If it wasn't for the war, how could I ever have been here?

DAISY: Why shouldn't you?

GATSBY: In the end, I know that. Here, or in places like this, all this is part of the thing I am going to win, but the war brought it to me sooner, that's all.

DAISY: I don't see why you shouldn't have as much as anyone.

GATSBY: I'm going to have as much — but it's all new to me. You are the first girl of your class I have ever really known.

DAISY: Not truly?

GATSBY: Oh, I have met plenty of others, but always with some indiscernible barbed wire between us.

DAISY: All that sort of thing doesn't seem to matter any more.

James Rennie and Florence Eldridge as Gatsby and Daisy.

GATSBY: When I first came here, with the other boys from
   Camp Taylor, I was afraid. I had never been in such a beautiful
   house before, but that didn't frighten me as much as the
   thought that you lived here.

DAISY: I don't see why you had to be afraid of that.

GATSBY: All this meant no more to you than my cot out at
the Camp meant to me — but to me there was mystery here ...
a feeling of stepping into a world that was strange, and yet
familiar, a hint of romances, of gaiety — a hint of bedrooms
upstairs more beautiful and cool than any other rooms, of
great high ceilinged rooms, and then there was you.

DAISY: And you wanted me? I am glad.

GATSBY: Every man who ever saw you must have you, and
most of them had something to offer. I know that, I know
my being here was just an accident, just this war, just this
uniform! I am not afraid for a minute for my future, dear, but
I haven't any past.

DAISY: I don't want you to have any past longer ago than
just the month I've known you. You'll do big things and
you'll come back to me a famous man! You've never told me
anything about your people and I don't care! I'd just like to
know if you have a father and mother alive, that's all.

GATSBY: Yes, they are alive.

DAISY: You never talk of them.

GATSBY: Somehow, I don't know, they never seemed to be
my father and mother at all. They did the best they could,
I suppose, but they never had much time for me, and so I had
to dream out a father and a mother for myself, just as I had
to dream out a whole life for myself. I wasn't happy ever.
Whenever anyone of those around me guessed at the big hopes
I had, the visions of a future, they laughed.

DAISY: You must have been a funny little boy!

GATSBY: I hid myself away. I used to lay awake at night, when
no one could bother me, then a whole great beautiful world
spun itself out for me, and I built my castles in the moonlight
of my garret window. I learned to believe in myself.

DAISY: Oh, I guess you believe in yourself all right.

GATSBY: I always did until I met you, and then not again until last night.

DAISY: But why?

GATSBY: I was afraid the invisible cloak of this uniform of mine might slip from my shoulders and I would hear someone say "What are you doing here in her house?" And then last night, you gave yourself to me, and now all my dreams are gone.

DAISY: I should think that after — after — last night all your dreams would have been more beautiful than ever.

GATSBY: They were selfish dreams, dreams of a future, of big things ... they don't matter now.

DAISY: Are you sure?

GATSBY: Tonight, with you in my arms, I gave up everything but just to live for you. That is what I was saying to myself when you moved and looked up at me and asked me what I was thinking when I kissed your hair.

DAISY: That you were giving up everything you had dreamt about, just to dream about me!

GATSBY: I gave them up the first night, out there by the gate.

DAISY: I know the night you mean.

GATSBY: The quiet lights of the house were humming out into the darkness and there seemed to be a stir and bustle among the stars. I could see, out of the corner of my eye, the blocks of the sidewalks in the moonlight and I had the fancy that they formed a ladder that mounted to a secret place above the trees. I knew that I could climb to it, if I climbed alone, but my arms were around you and my heart beat faster and faster as your white face came up to mine. I knew that when I kissed

14

you all that I had meant to live for would go, and just your image would take its place, and so I hesitated.

DAISY *(hurt)*: Oh no!

GATSBY: For a moment, to listen just once more to the tuning fork I had struck upon a star, then — I kissed you, and as my lips touched yours you blossomed for me like a flower.

(Sally enters anxiously)

SALLY: Miss Daisy! Yo' Ma is gettin' awful nervous like! Dey is somebody in there she wants you to see and she's just a telephoning and a telephoning and a carryin' on something terrible!

GATSBY: All right, Sally.

DAISY *(clings to him)*: I don't want you to go.

GATSBY *(looks at watch)*: I can just make camp by twelve. I can't be late, you know.

DAISY: You must go, of course.

SALLY: Yo' Ma might come in here any minute, you know.

GATSBY: Just one minute! Then come back to her.

SALLY: Yes sir — just you see it's a real minute!

GATSBY: It's goodbye.

DAISY: I am afraid! I'll be all alone! I am not strong, I'm not brave. I am afraid of mother! I am afraid of the way I have to live — there is such a crowd always, and so much to do — I don't see why you have to go away and leave me!

GATSBY: So that I can come back and take you!

DAISY: I don't want to be left alone! People make me do things. We ought to have been married, really married! I wish I hadn't said no!

GATSBY: You may have been right, what difference does it make? You couldn't have been any more mine than you are — nobody can take you away from me now!

DAISY: It's too hard! To be so happy for just a little while. How long are you going to be gone? How long is the war going to last? How do I know! I think I must have been crazy to make myself unhappy when I didn't have to be.

GATSBY: You couldn't help what has happened any more than I could have helped it. That's the big thing — not the way we have to live for awhile, not even the war, just that! The war will end, I'll come back for you and you will be waiting for me.

(Sally enters)

SALLY: You all must go! She'll be in here sure! Dey will be an awful lot of trouble!

GATSBY *(with his arms about Daisy)*:   You will love me?

DAISY: I can't help loving you!

GATSBY: Goodbye.

DAISY: No! No!

GATSBY: I must! *(he kisses her)*

DAISY: Not yet!

SALLY: Now, Miss Daisy.

DAISY: I don't want you to go!

GATSBY: I'll come back! Don't be afraid of that. I am going to do things, big things, for you.

DAISY: You may be killed!

GATSBY: No, not while you belong to me. Goodbye, dear. Take her, Sally.

DAISY: No! No!

SALLY: Now, now. Now, my baby.

GATSBY: Goodbye.

(He puts her into Sally's arms and exits — Sally puts her into chair)

SALLY: I don't know what's been goin' on here! I don't know what troubles you all has got yourself into but for the Lord's sake, baby, stop your cryin' and get yourself fixed before yo' Ma catches us!

DAISY: I don't care! I don't care what happens!

(The door opens and Mrs. Fay enters)

MRS. FAY: Daisy!

SALLY: It's all right, Miss Amy. I swear to God dat everything is all right, she is just a little bit nervous like and upset about something, dat is all!

MRS. FAY: Go away, Sally.

SALLY: Jes' a little bit nervous like!

MRS. FAY: Go away!

SALLY: Yes, Miss Amy.

(She exits)

MRS. FAY: Daisy!

DAISY: You mustn't talk to me tonight. You mustn't do it!

MRS. FAY *(quietly)*:   Listen to me, Daisy. Tom Buchanan is here.

DAISY: I won't see him! You can't make me see him!

MRS. FAY: He came all the way from New York just to see you.

DAISY: I don't care! He might have known I didn't want to see him.

MRS. FAY: How? In the spring you were all but engaged to him. You have been writing to him all summer.

DAISY: It's different now!

MRS. FAY: Because of this Lieutenant Gatsby?

DAISY: Yes.

MRS. FAY: He is going in the morning.

DAISY: You know that?

MRS. FAY: Yes. That is all I know, all that I care to know, we are not going to talk about him any more, Daisy — he has gone to the war like thousands of other young men — just as Tom is going — you said goodbye to him, didn't you? I mean to Lieutenant Gatsby?

DAISY: Yes.

MRS. FAY: That's all I ask you to do for Tom Buchanan, he is an old friend.

DAISY (reluctantly): Yes.

MRS. FAY: I'll bring him to you.

DAISY: I wish you wouldn't, mother. Not tonight.

MRS. FAY: Don't be silly! I'll give you a minute, dear, to fix your hair and to powder your nose. You've been crying.

DAISY: I don't care. I tell you I don't want to see him!

MRS. FAY: All right, I'll give you just a minute.

(Mrs. Fay exits. Daisy sobs a moment and wipes her eyes, then takes a vanity case and fixes her hair in the little mirror and powders her face. As the door opens she puts the vanity case away and hastily rises)

DAISY: Oh!

(As Mrs. Fay enters with Tom Buchanan, a big, powerful young fellow in Captain's uniform)

MRS. FAY (at door): Here is Tom!

TOM: Hello, Daisy. It's great to see you again!

DAISY: Hello, Tom.

(She crosses and takes his hand)

You were a sweet old thing to come way down here to see me, before you went away!

(She smiles up at him. Now in the middle distance an army band plays "Tipperary")

CURTAIN

ACT I

SCENE

Nick Carraway's cottage at West Egg, Long Island.
August, 1925.

A pretty modern cottage with door down left to bedroom, door up left to a small veranda and open French windows at back right center. Through these windows one sees a garden, and back of that a view of Long Island Sound with a distant shore line across the water.

Nick Carraway, a young fellow about twenty-five, sits at right reading a paper. He is dressed in afternoon sports clothes and smokes a cigarette. From outside at left comes the sound of an automobile horn, which is repeated several times. Nick rises impatiently and steps through the window at back onto the veranda and looks out left.

NICK: Hello there! What is it? What are you making all that row about?

(A voice is heard in answer but the words are not distinct)

What? Where's what? Speak English! Oh — all right. Now what can I do for you?

(Meyer Wolfshiem enters on veranda at back, he is a well-dressed Jew of middle age; he speaks with a natural Jewish dialect)

MEYER: I vonted to know if somebody couldn't tell me the vay to the Gatsby place!

NICK: That's it ...

(They are standing together by the open French windows)

right next door.

MEYER: But there is a hedge there. How do you get in?

NICK: You don't; you'll have to back out. You took the wrong turn about a hundred yards back there.

MEYER *(looks right)*: I never been to Gatsby's place yet, it's wonderful!

NICK: A conservative remark.

MEYER: Eh?

NICK: It is, as you said, quite wonderful!

MEYER: Of course you know Gatsby?

NICK: Yes.

MEYER: Everybody knows Gatsby. He's a friend of mine.

NICK: Really?

MEYER: Yes. One of the finest young men I know.

NICK: Then you are well acquainted with him.

MEYER: A long time! I met him just after the war.

NICK: Really?

MEYER: I knew I'd met a man of fine breeding after I had talked to him for an hour. I said to myself, here's the kind of man it would be a pleasure to take home and introduce to your mother and sister! High class! I see you're looking at my cuff buttons.

NICK: Excuse me!

MEYER: They ain't a secret! See? Finest specimens of human molars.

NICK *(coldly)*:   A very interesting idea!

MEYER: Yeah. Gatsby is my friend. I'm proud to tell it. He's a gentleman. He's got manners, and he's very careful about women, he would never so much as look at a friend's wife. You know him pretty well?

NICK: Not very. I have only recently taken this cottage — it's a very simple shabby little place, as you see — the great Mr. Gatsby is my neighbor, we've met, that's about all.

(Mrs. Morton, an elderly housekeeper, enters from hall and puts some letters on table)

MEYER: You got a nice little place here, only maybe it would be better if the grass was cut a little.

NICK: That's possible. You will have to back your car as far as the gate, then turn to your right.

MEYER: I'm much obliged, Mr. —

NICK: Carraway.

MEYER: Mr. Carraway. Anybody that's a friend of Mr. Gatsby's is all right with me. My name is Wolfshiem, Meyer Wolfshiem.

NICK: Ah!

MEYER: Yes sir, glad to have met you Mr. Carraway.

(He exits)

(Nick turns down to center stage, speaking to Mrs. Morton)

NICK: Another lost soul looking for the great Gatsby!

MRS. MORTON: Two letters, sir.

NICK: Thanks.

(He takes the letters and as he opens them a sound of a lawn mower is heard outside)

What's that?

(He glances out the window)

MRS. MORTON: It's a man cutting the grass, sir.

NICK: What man?

MRS. MORTON: One of Mr. Gatsby's gardeners, he said Mr. Gatsby sent him.

NICK: Well I'll be damned!

MRS. MORTON: Yes sir, I didn't see what harm it could do to cut it.

NICK: I suppose not. I am giving a little tea this afternoon you know, Mrs. Morton.

MRS. MORTON: Yes sir, I'm sure I'll do the best I can.

NICK: And one of my guests is to be the great Gatsby himself.

MRS. MORTON *(alarmed)*: Mr. Gatsby!

NICK: Yes — he sent over for me night before last, after you had gone for the day, and asked me to one of his parties.

MRS. MORTON: Was it very wild, sir?

NICK: I thought it rather stupid, but I hate all that sort of thing.

MRS. MORTON: I'd be afraid of him!

NICK: Gatsby? He seemed rather a decent sort.

MRS. MORTON: They say he killed a man once!

NICK: Bosh!

MRS. MORTON: The grocer at the village says he knows for a fact that Mr. Gatsby was a German spy during the war.

NICK: He was in the American army during the war — I know that for a fact.

MRS. MORTON: I see him often, out at the end of his little dock there, looking out across the bay. I see him there most every night when I'm on my way home. If you could see the look on his face, sir, the way I have. I guess you'd believe he killed somebody!

(Ryan, a butler, comes to the open window at back followed by two footmen in grand livery; one footman has his arms full of hot house flowers, the other has a very large tray covered by a cloth)

RYAN: I beg your pardon, sir. From Mr. Gatsby.

NICK: What?

RYAN: Some flowers, sir, and some little things for the tea.

NICK: Oh, take care of them, Mrs. Morton.

MRS. MORTON: Yes sir, bring them this way please.

RYAN *(to footmen)*: This way.

(Mrs. Morton, Ryan and the footmen exit to hall. Nick lights a cigarette and sits and reads his two letters. Gatsby enters on the veranda and comes to window)

GATSBY: Is everything all right, Mr. Carraway?

NICK: Hello, oh, it's you, Gatsby. Come in.

GATSBY *(enters)*: I just wanted to know if everything was all right.

NICK *(glances out window)*: The grass looks fine, if that's what you mean.

GATSBY: What grass? Oh, your lawn, yes, it looks very well.

NICK: And you sent something on a tray.

GATSBY: You're not offended?

NICK: Not at all, it is, of course, in a way, your party.

GATSBY: It's a big service you are doing me.

NICK: Why? I telephoned my cousin on my return from Louisville, I wanted her to see this little place. I just happened to mention that a man named Gatsby was my neighbor and she said she had once known a man named Gatsby.

GATSBY: Yes, I knew your cousin before her marriage.

NICK: She said she'd like to meet you, and I fixed today.

GATSBY: Her husband, Mr. Buchanan, is coming with her.

NICK *(surprised)*:   You don't mean Daisy phoned you?

GATSBY: No, Jordan Baker did.

NICK: Jordan Baker?

GATSBY: She was down there resting up for her tournament tomorrow, she's playing up in Westchester.

NICK: Oh! The Jordan Baker?

GATSBY: Yes.

NICK: So she's a pal of Daisy's! Pretty girl, by her photos; weren't there some rather nasty stories about her?

GATSBY: There was a scandal at her first big golf tournament, but it was hushed up.

NICK: I remember hearing something.

GATSBY: A caddy claimed he saw her move her ball from a bad lie in the semi-finals, but he retracted I believe; anyway it blew over. She's a great golfer and a pretty woman.

NICK: But not exactly on the level.

GATSBY: We can't quite expect real loyalty from women, can we old man? You can't blame them too much for breaking faith.

NICK: Why should a woman break faith any more than a man?

GATSBY: They get pushed about more I think, pushed in directions they never meant to go at all.

NICK: Possibly.

GATSBY *(at window)*:   Oh yes, old sport! Your cousin's house is over there, across the bay. You can see it from this window.

NICK: That so? I never located it.

GATSBY: Yes — I wonder if you'd be offended if I were to say something to you?

NICK: Something?

GATSBY: You don't make very much money, do you?

NICK: No, not very much.

GATSBY: I thought you didn't, if you'll pardon my — you see, I carry on a little business on the side, a sort of side line, you understand. And I thought if you don't make very much — you're selling bonds, aren't you, old sport?

NICK: Trying to.

GATSBY: Well, this would interest you. It wouldn't take up much of your time, and you might pick up a nice bit of money. It happens to be a rather confidential sort of thing.

NICK *(coldly)*:   I've got my hands full. I'm much obliged, but I couldn't take on any more work.

(He speaks a little curtly)

GATSBY: Oh, it's all right, if that's what you mean. Of course I know you're a gentleman. I wouldn't offer you anything that wasn't right.

NICK: Thanks, but my time is fully taken up.

GATSBY: It's up to you, of course.

NICK: By the way there was a man looking for you, a friend of yours he said, he drove in here by mistake.

GATSBY: I'll have a sign put up, sorry to be such a bother. The man didn't give his name, did he?

NICK: Wolfshiem.

GATSBY: Oh! Meyer Wolfshiem! Yes, in a way he is a friend
of mine. He is quite a character around New York, or rather
along Broadway.

NICK: Who is he anyhow, an actor?

GATSBY: No.

NICK: A dentist?

GATSBY: Meyer Wolfshiem! No, he's a gambler. He's the man
who fixed the World's Series back in 1919.

NICK: Fixed the World's Series?

GATSBY: Yes.

NICK: That's a queer thing to think about! It never occurred
to me that one man could deliberately set out to play with the
faith of fifty million people with the single-mindedness of a
burglar blowing a safe. Why isn't he in jail?

GATSBY: They can't get him, old sport, he's a smart man.

NICK: So it seems.

(He turns away coldly)

GATSBY *(after a pause during which he looks closely at
Nick)*:   Look here, old sport, what's your opinion of me
anyhow?

NICK: My opinion — really, we've hardly met —

GATSBY: Well, I'm going to tell you something about myself.
I don't want you to get a wrong idea of me from all these
stories you hear.

NICK: They are a bit picturesque.

GATSBY: I'll tell you God's truth!

(He starts to lie in a rather set and calculated manner)

I am the son of some wealthy people in the middle west, all
dead now. I was brought up in America, but educated at

Oxford, because all my ancestors have been educated there for many years. It's a family tradition.

(Nick thinks he is a liar and looks at him with a half scornful smile)

NICK: What part of the middle west?

GATSBY: Oh — Michigan. My family all died and I came in for a good deal of money.

NICK: You're lucky.

GATSBY: After that I lived like a young rajah in all the capitals of Europe, Paris, Venice, Rome, collecting jewels, chiefly rubies, hunting big game, painting a little and trying to forget something very sad that had happened to me long ago.

NICK: Oh!

(He is a bit dazed by all this)

GATSBY: Then came the war, old sport. It was a great relief, and I tried hard to die, but I seemed to bear an enchanted life, at the end I was a Major and every allied government gave me a decoration, even little Montenegro — Look — that's the one from Montenegro.

(He takes a bit of metal on a ribbon from his pocket)

NICK *(reads the inscription)*:   "Orderi de Danilo, Montenegro, Nicolas Rex."

GATSBY: Turn it.

NICK *(reads)*:   "Major Jay Gatsby, For Valour Extraordinary."

GATSBY: I've a whole case of them in my library.

NICK: My cousin's husband was a Major too, Tom Buchanan. Did you ever know him?

GATSBY: No — Jordan Baker telephoned me that she and Mr. Buchanan would bring her here — bring Mrs. Buchanan here I mean, then drive on up to town.

NICK: Yes.

(He goes to the window as Mrs. Morton enters with bowls of Gatsby's flowers)

They should be here now.

GATSBY: I am going back for a few moments, to see Meyer Wolfshiem, you know. Of course you won't wait tea for me.

NICK: No, but in a way it's your party.

GATSBY: I may not be able to get back before Mr. Buchanan and Miss Baker go, but you might say to your cousin that I will surely come.

NICK: I hope so, she seemed anxious to meet you.

GATSBY: Yes, I'll surely come.

(He exits to veranda and off)

MRS. MORTON: I don't know, when you look at him you can't help thinking that maybe he <u>did</u> kill somebody!

NICK: I can't make him out. He isn't altogether a liar, and yet there is something wrong.

MRS. MORTON: He gives terrible parties — actresses and worse! The carryings on are a scandal. Do you know what he's got? A machine run by electricity just to squeeze oranges! Human hands couldn't do it fast enough.

(An automobile horn outside)

NICK: See who it is, Mrs. Morton.

MRS. MORTON: Yes, sir.

(She looks about the room)

I do hope everything is all right.

(She exits)

(Daisy Buchanan, the Daisy Fay of the prologue, runs in on veranda)

DAISY: Nick! You didn't think I'd wait to have you open any old doors for me!

NICK: Hello, Daisy.

DAISY *(quickly)*: Tom is only going to stay a minute. Don't say a word to him about — about anyone else being here for tea.

NICK: Meaning Gatsby?

DAISY *(startled)*: He isn't here now, is he?

NICK *(smiles)*: No. I have an idea he won't be here until Tom goes.

DAISY: So much the better — now don't look shocked! It's just an old friend, I haven't even seen him since early in the war.

NICK: Oh, I don't know that I am easily shocked, anyway I guess you are safe enough, Daisy, with Tom, and the kid and everything.

DAISY: A staid old married woman on the shelf ages and ages and ages ago.

(Mrs. Morton opens the door and Tom Buchanan enters with Jordan Baker. Tom is older than when we saw him in the prologue — heavier and coarser. Jordan Baker is a tall, slight, athletic girl).

TOM: Hello, Nick! Haven't seen you for three months.

NICK: Hello.

DAISY: This is Jordan Baker, Nick, of course you've heard about her.

NICK: Of course I have.

JORDAN *(shakes hands)*: I'm paralyzed with happiness!

NICK: To meet me? Why?

JORDAN: I don't know. I always say that.

DAISY: He's been in Louisville since I've seen him, Jordan. Tell us all about it, Nick.

NICK: About the same.

DAISY: Do they miss me?

NICK: The whole town is desolate. All the cars have the left rear wheel painted black as a mourning wreath, and there's a persistent wail all night along the avenues.

DAISY: How gorgeous! Let's go back, Tom — tomorrow!

(Mrs. Morton enters with tea and cakes on a tray; on this tray is also a bowl of ice, and glasses and bottles of charged water. Mrs. Morton puts this tray down on the table near Daisy)

Oh! Cakes! Wonderful cakes!

(Nick gets bottle of Scotch whiskey from cabinet)

NICK: Here's some fairly decent Scotch.

JORDAN: Tea for me, I am playing tomorrow and I want to win. I'm absolutely in training.

DAISY: Of course you'll win. Tea for me too.

TOM: Scotch for me!

(Daisy pours tea. Nick gives the whiskey to Tom and takes some himself)

DAISY: Where did you get these marvelous cakes?

NICK: They came from a sort of fairy godmother, or you might say a kind of a genie.

DAISY: A caterer?

NICK: No — a magician! He waves his hand and there are cakes.

DAISY *(with tea cup)*: There! Look at my finger!

JORDAN: What about it?

DAISY: It's all bruised. You did it, Tom. I know you didn't mean to, but you <u>did</u> it. That's what I get for marrying a brute of a man — a great, big, hulking physical specimen of a —

TOM *(angry)*:   I hate that word hulking, even in kidding!

DAISY *(spitefully)*:   Hulking!

(Mrs. Morton exits)

Florence Eldridge as Daisy and Catherine Willard as Jordan.

NICK: Don't row, Daisy. Can't you talk about crops or something? You make me feel uncivilized.

TOM: Civilization is going to pieces! I've gotten to be a terrible pessimist about things.

DAISY: Tom's getting very profound. He reads deep books with long words in them.

TOM *(earnestly)*:   Kidding aside, we are all Nordics. I am and you are —

DAISY: I want to be one too!

TOM: We've produced all the things that go to make civilization. Oh — science and art, and all that. Do you see?

DAISY *(to Nick)*: I'll tell you a family secret, it's about our chauffeur's nose.

TOM: There's a man named Goddard who wrote a book —

DAISY: He wasn't always a chauffeur, he used to be the silver polisher for a family that had a silver service for two hundred people.

TOM *(annoyed)*: Just a minute, Daisy!

DAISY: He had to polish it from morning until night until finally it began to affect his nose.

JORDAN: Things went from bad to worse.

DAISY: Until one day —

TOM: Are we going to talk sense or —

(Mrs. Morton enters)

MRS. MORTON: I beg your pardon but there is somebody on the telephone asking for Mr. Buchanan.

DAISY *(coldly)*: Oh!

TOM: For me?

MRS. MORTON: Yes, sir.

TOM *(to Nick)*: Sorry, old man but — I gave your number, it's about a car I'm having repaired, it's rather important.

MRS. MORTON: The telephone is in the hall.

TOM: Thanks. I won't be a minute.

(He exits with Mrs. Morton)

JORDAN: Tell us a little more about the silver polisher, Daisy.

DAISY: No —

(She looks angrily toward the door)

Tom is always having trouble with his cars, you know.
I wonder if you two would mind if I helped him see to it.

(She exits to hall closing the door. Nick looks after her in surprise)

JORDAN: Well?

NICK: What is it?

JORDAN: Of course she'd shut the door! I'd like to hear what happens.

NICK: Is something happening?

JORDAN: You mean to say you don't know? I thought everybody knew.

NICK: I don't.

JORDAN: Tom's got some woman in New York.

NICK: Got some woman?

JORDAN: She might have the decency not to telephone him at a stranger's house.

NICK: It might have been anybody.

JORDAN: You saw how she looked.

NICK: She couldn't have <u>known</u>!

JORDAN: She's no fool! It would serve him right if she made it up with Gatsby.

NICK: Made up what? What are you talking about?

JORDAN: But surely you know that! You've asked them here, both of them.

NICK: I mentioned Gatsby's name. Daisy said she wanted to meet him; that's all I know.

JORDAN: Oh! Of course, I may be wrong, but I thought —

NICK: Thought what? I wish you'd tell me! She's my cousin, you know, and I don't quite know what to think of this Gatsby.

JORDAN: Nobody else does.

NICK: He's too damned romantic, and he talks like a copy book, and any fool can see he's a liar, yet there is something about him that gets you.

JORDAN: The women are mad about him. All of them, including me!

NICK: You know him?

JORDAN: Oh yes — I've been to his parties, and I met him once before, ages ago, but he doesn't remember that.

NICK: Tell me!

JORDAN: It's quite a pretty story, of course I haven't any business to tell it, but I'm sure I could tell it beautifully!

NICK: I'll be the judge of that.

JORDAN: Will you have it with frills or without?

NICK: With, but hurry up, before they get back.

JORDAN: Don't worry! Daisy will start something — we've plenty of time.

NICK: When did you meet this Gatsby?

JORDAN *(with a manner)*: In Louisville, one fall day in nineteen seventeen —

NICK *(alarmed)*: Not too many frills.

JORDAN: I was walking from one place to another, half on the sidewalk, and half on the lawns. I was happier on the lawns because I had on shoes from England with rubber nobs on the soles that bit into the soft ground.

NICK: Is that memory or descriptive detail?

JORDAN: I had on a new plaid skirt also, that blew a little in the wind, and whenever this happened the red, white and blue banners in front of all the houses stretched out stiff and said "tut-tut-tut" in a disapproving way.

NICK: War time?

JORDAN: Daisy was the belle of Louisville, and all day long the telephone rang in her house and excited young officers from Camp Taylor ran back and forth and fought for every minute of her time.

NICK: And Gatsby?

JORDAN: Was one of them. She introduced me to him one day on the street. He was looking at her in a way every young girl wants to be looked at some time, and because it seemed so romantic to me I have remembered it ever since. Of course I was just a kid.

NICK: You met him only once?

JORDAN: That's all, two days after that one of the boys at the Camp told me his regiment was on the way, and I didn't see much of Daisy after that.

NICK: Why?

JORDAN: She didn't play about much; there were rumors. I was told something about a big row when her mother found her packing a bag to go to New York to say goodbye to a soldier who was going overseas — of course she didn't go — but she kept out of things all that winter, and it was two years before I saw much of her again.

NICK: Her baby is three? She and Tom have been married —

JORDAN: About four years. I was one of her bridesmaids. Tom gave her a string of pearls worth three hundred thousand! It was a big wedding.

NICK: I heard all about it.

JORDAN: Here's something you never heard. I came into her room half an hour before the bridal dinner and found her lying on her bed as lovely as a June night in her flowered dress, and as drunk as a monkey.

NICK: No!

JORDAN: She had a bottle of Sauterne in one hand and a soldier's letter in the other. "Gratulate me," she said, "I never had a drink before, but oh how I do enjoy it." I was scared, I can tell you; it was the first time I had ever seen a girl like that.

NICK: Was there a row?

JORDAN: Just with her mother. Daisy cried and swore she wouldn't go through with the wedding, but of course she did — her mother and a cold bath and some spirits of ammonia fixed everything — everyone said she was the prettiest bride of the year — and that's my story!

NICK: Why didn't you keep it to yourself? Now I'm damned if I know what to do.

JORDAN: There's gratitude — of all the —

(The door opens and Daisy enters; she has been crying. Tom follows sulky and upset)

Well, that car's all fixed by this time I suppose?

DAISY *(angrily)*: I am going to stay here with you tonight, Nick. You can get some chaperone in if being cousins isn't enough. I won't go home.

TOM: For God's sake, Daisy, don't make a scene!

DAISY: You can put that man out! I know perfectly well why you keep him. Tell him to go away and take that wife of his with him. If he's there tonight I won't be.

TOM: Can't we settle this between ourselves?

DAISY: It isn't between ourselves. It's between you and me and our chauffeur's wife. Get rid of them, or get rid of me. Take your choice.

TOM: You might have decency enough not to discuss this in public.

DAISY: Decency! Are you trying to make me laugh? Anyway, Nick is my cousin and Jordan is a pal.

(She turns to them)

She called him up here. She was to send him word, he says, about his car. The chauffeur's wife! About his car.

TOM: Damn me if I'll stand much more of this.

DAISY: You won't see me again while that woman is on the place. If Nick won't take me in I'll find someone who will.

NICK: Easy, Daisy!

TOM: How can I get rid of him? Do you want me to tell him he's fired because you're jealous of his wife?

DAISY: If you won't discharge him I will, and I'll tell him why too! People are laughing at me, as you know. Laughing at me! Damn me if I'll stand for it!

(She crosses furiously out on the veranda and calls)

Wilson! Come here, Wilson!

TOM: Are you crazy?

DAISY: You tell him or I will! I won't have that wife of his in my house another night!

(Wilson, a chauffeur, enters to the French windows at back. He is a pale, slight, threatening looking fellow of thirty)

WILSON: Yes, Mrs. Buchanan.

TOM *(hastily)*:   We — we have made other arrangements about — about the car, you know, something has come up that — that makes it necessary to make a change.

WILSON: I don't understand! There's a lot of things been going on lately that I don't understand.

(He looks defiantly at Tom)

TOM: I'm not going to keep you, that's all. I've made up my mind that I don't need but one man, and Scott has been with me for years.

WILSON (*bitterly*): Sudden, isn't it?

NICK: Not at all. Mr. Buchanan happened to mention that he really didn't need you, and I said that in that case I thought I could find you a very good place.

WILSON: What place?

NICK: With a very wealthy neighbor of mine, a Mr. Gatsby.

TOM: Gatsby? Who's Gatsby?

DAISY (*quickly*): What does it matter who he is, if he has money and wants a chauffeur?

NICK: He lives next door, in the big house. I'll speak to him tonight. You see him first thing in the morning.

TOM: See him this afternoon if you want to. I'll drive Miss Baker up to town, you hang around here until I come back for Mrs. Buchanan. That's all, bring the car around to the door.

WILSON: Yes, sir.

(He looks at Tom coldly and exits)

TOM (*to Daisy*): Now I hope you're satisfied.

DAISY: Oh, I'll make a bluff if you will, but this thing was getting just a little bit too raw.

(She turns to Nick)

Nice people, aren't we, Nick? Aren't you glad you're a bachelor? Look at him, Jordan. The poor man is actually blushing.

JORDAN: Is he? I didn't know people did that any more.

(She looks at her wrist watch)

Take me up to town, Tom. I've a million things to do.

ToM: All right.

JORDAN: Goodbye, Mr. Carraway.

(Offers her hand)

See you anon.

DAISY: Of course you will. In fact I think I'll arrange
a marriage. Come around often, Nick, and I'll sort of,
oh, fling you together. You know – lock you up in linen
closets and push you out to sea in a boat — and all that sort
of thing.

JORDAN:

(crosses to door)

Goodbye — I haven't heard a word.

ToM: I'll be back about seven.

DAISY *(coldly)*:   Yes, don't do too much telephoning on the
way.

JORDAN: See you Saturday.

DAISY: Don't forget!

(Tom and Jordan exit)

NICK: She's a nice girl.

DAISY: She's a terrible liar and they say she's a bum sport, but
I like her.

NICK: From Louisville, she said?

DAISY: Yes, our white girlhood was passed together, our
beautiful white girlhood! Ha! Ha! Ha! Oh God! How tired I
am of everything!

NICK: Take it easy, have a drink or something.

DAISY *(sits)*:   Oh, I'm all right, you just aren't used to me.
We don't know each other so very well, Nick, even if we are
cousins. You didn't even come to my wedding.

NICK: I wasn't back from the war.

DAISY: That's true. Well, I've had a very bad time, Nick, and I'm pretty cynical about everything.

NICK: You've got a nice kid.

DAISY: Yes — let me tell you what I said when she was born; would you like to hear?

NICK: Very much.

DAISY: It will show you how I've gotten to feel about things. Well — my baby was less than an hour old and Tom was God knows where. I woke up out of the ether with an utterly abandoned feeling, and asked the nurse right away if it was a boy or a girl. She told me it was a girl, and so I turned my head away and cried. "All right," I said, "I'm glad it's a girl, and I hope she'll be a fool, that's the best thing a girl can be in this world, a beautiful little fool."

NICK: Don't cry, Daisy.

DAISY: You see, I've gotten to think everything is terrible anyhow. Everybody thinks so, the most advanced people. And I <u>know</u>. I've been everywhere, and seen everything — and done everything! Sophisticated. God, I'm sophisticated!

NICK: Daisy ...

DAISY: Well?

NICK: Gatsby will be here in a moment, you haven't forgotten him?

DAISY: I am a fool to see him and ten times bigger fool to let him see me. Eight years! We're not the same people. I thought there would be a thrill in it — it's fun to play with fire — but it just gets you in a mess to play with ashes.

NICK (*up by the window looking off*): He's coming, Daisy.

DAISY: At that I might as well powder my nose.

NICK: And bathe your eyes, you've been crying.

(He crosses left and opens door of bedroom)

In here.

DAISY: We're damned fools, Nick dear, all of us.

(She exits to bedroom. Nick shuts the door and crosses to the French windows and stands waiting. Gatsby enters; he has changed to rather formal afternoon dress)

NICK *(looks at him)*:   Good God! Are you going to a funeral?

GATSBY: Is —

(He looks about)

NICK: She's here.

GATSBY: Oh — here! It's the funniest thing, old sport, I can't — when I try —

(He turns away)

NICK: She'll be here in a minute.

GATSBY *(afraid)*:   This is a terrible mistake, old sport, a terrible mistake.

NICK: You're just embarrassed, that's all. Daisy is embarrassed too.

GATSBY: She's embarrassed?

NICK: Just as much as you are.

GATSBY: It might be better for me to go.

NICK: You're acting like a little boy. You can't go.

GATSBY: No, I can't go. I have been waiting quite a long time for this, you know.

NICK: No, I didn't know.

GATSBY: We — we're good friends. I'd been to her house, you know, and things like that; she had a fine house. I'd like to have her see mine.

(He looks out window)

It looks well, doesn't it?

NICK: Of course it does! It's a palace!

GATSBY: It took me just three years to earn the money that bought it.

NICK: I thought you inherited your money?

GATSBY: Oh — yes — but I lost most of it in the big panic, the panic of the war.

NICK: In the market?

GATSBY: It doesn't matter — I mean — you see I've been in several things. I was in the drug business, and then I was in the oil business, but I'm not in either one now.

NICK: Just a minute.

(He crosses and raps smartly on door of room L)

Daisy! Mr. Gatsby is here.

(He turns on Gatsby)

You're not to run away, you know.

GATSBY: No, I won't run away.

(The door opens and Daisy enters — all three are much affected but Daisy is in far better control than either of the others)

DAISY: Mr. Gatsby!

(She crosses)

I certainly am awfully glad to see you.

(Gatsby is standing with his hand resting on the mantelpiece, his hand moves convulsively and strikes against a clock. Nick puts out his hand and steadies the clock)

NICK: Look out!

GATSBY: I — I'm sorry about the clock.

NICK: It's all right.

GATSBY: I — I'm sorry about the clock.

NICK: It's an old clock.

DAISY: We haven't met for many years.

NICK: I know.

(He crosses up stage to window)

GATSBY: Where are you going?

NICK: I'll be back.

(He exits)

DAISY: He's — he's my cousin.

GATSBY: Yes, he said he was.

DAISY: My cousin.

GATSBY: Yes, I know.

DAISY: He didn't live in Louisville.

GATSBY: No — I — I didn't think he did.

DAISY: It's queer, your meeting him.

GATSBY: We live next door, you see.

(He points out window)

That's my place, over there.

DAISY: All that?

GATSBY: Yes, do you like it?

DAISY: I love it! It looks like the World's Fair.

GATSBY: My view is the same as this. If it wasn't for the mist you could see your home, across the bay. You always have a green light that burns all night at the end of your dock.

DAISY: You found out where I live?

GATSBY: That's why I bought this place, so that I could see the lights of your windows.

DAISY *(turns away)*: Don't — make me — cry.

GATSBY: No — I didn't mean that at all — I am happy — when I see them.

DAISY: I haven't been happy — ever!

GATSBY *(gently)*: It wasn't right, to make you marry him. I know she made you — your mother.

DAISY: I don't know, things happen.

GATSBY: The last letters you wrote — I knew something was forcing you away from me. I wanted to come to you, anybody would understand that, but we were in the Argonne battles, and of course I could — I got your mother's letter the day I was made a Major and put in command of the Divisional Machine Guns.

DAISY: I should have written. I always was a coward.

GATSBY: When I came back you were on your wedding trip.

DAISY: You must hate me.

GATSBY: No — I got down to Louisville on the last of my army pay. I stayed there a week, walking the streets where our footsteps had clicked together those September nights, revisiting the out of the way places you had taken me in your little white car.

DAISY: I knew, always, what it meant to you.

GATSBY: Your house had seemed to me more mysterious and gay than any other house — and the city seemed to me like that, because you had lived there. The day I left I had a feeling that it was you I was leaving behind me — although, of course, I knew I had lost you long before. I stood out on the open vestibule as the station slid away, and I stretched out my hand desperately as if to snatch a wisp of air, as if to save a fragment of the spot you had made so lovely.

(She drops her head; he stands beside her with his hand on the back of her chair as Nick enters briskly)

NICK: Well, you two! How about a little tea?

GATSBY *(turns to him):*   Why yes, old sport, why not? Let's have a little tea.

CURTAIN

ACT II

SCENE

Gatsby's library.

One week later.

This library is a great circular room with an enormous fireplace at room right. An arch to hall stage left and very high French windows onto a wide veranda, the veranda is circular, like the room, and it is gay with decorative lanterns etc. Between the fireplace and the windows, and between the door to hall and the windows, there are cases of well-bound books.

Back of the veranda railing there is a view of the Sound, and on the distant shore there are a few twinkling lights.

Meyer Wolfshiem and Gatsby are discovered with cigars and highballs, both are in evening dress.

MEYER: Everybody says it! Who's Gatsby? Do you know Gatsby? I'm proud you're my friend. You live good. Better than good. You live almost like a king.

GATSBY: All my life I meant to live like this.

MEYER: Well, now you're satisfied!

GATSBY: No.

MEYER: You ain't got all you want yet?

GATSBY: No.

MEYER: You'll get it.

GATSBY: Yes, by God, I'll get it!

MEYER: Only take it nice and easy. Lots of the boys I know got a good start, not so good as yours, but nice, but they pushed their luck, and something broke, somebody squealed maybe, or maybe it was a woman butted in, and where are they, up the river there, or even worse in Atlanta.

(Ryan, the butler, enters)

RYAN: Detroit on the wire, Mr. Gatsby. Will you take it here or in your study?

GATSBY: Here.

RYAN *(picks up phone)*: Mr. Gatsby is ready.

(He hands the phone to Gatsby)

GATSBY: Hello. Yes. No. No, he can't. He can't do that! Tell him so, and tell Katspaugh! Don't pay him a penny until he shuts his mouth! — No, he can't. We know too much about him, if he tries to threaten put the screws on. Yes. You don't have to call me again. You know what to do. That's all.

(He rings off)

MEYER: Any trouble?

GATSBY: Blakely in Detroit has been talking too much.

RYAN *(earnestly)*: He's a welcher, Mr. Gatsby, he always was. I told you that he was a stool in the old days for Bill Devery.

GATSBY: Bob will take care of him, it's all right. There is a lot of easy money around just now and some of the boys are losing their heads.

RYAN *(warning)*: Some one on the veranda, sir.

GATSBY: All right.

(He turns up and looks out)

Ah! Glad to see you, Mr. Carraway.

(Nick enters)

NICK: Good evening.

GATSBY *(alarmed)*: You're not alone?

NICK: My cousin and her husband and Miss Baker are at my house dressing, they are staying over the night with me. They will be over by the time the crowd gets here. Oh —

(as he sees Meyer)

Mr. Wolfshiem. Glad to see you.

MEYER: I'm proud! I see you in New York today.

NICK: I didn't see you.

MEYER: I was busy lookin' in a window, but I see you go past.

NICK: Window shopping?

MEYER: Thinking how old I was. It's funny almost! I was lookin' in the window of the old Metropole, Mr. Gatsby.

GATSBY: Oh?

MEYER: I ain't looked in it for a long time and it seemed full of faces dead and gone, full of friends, mostly gone. I can't forget so long as I live the night they shot Rosey Rosenthal there. It vos six of us at the table, and Rosey had eat and drunk a lot all evening. When it was almost morning the waiter came up to him with a funny look and says somebody wants to speak with him outside.

GATSBY: I remember hearing about it.

MEYER: "All right," says Rosey, and begins to get up, but I pulls him down in his chair, I says, "Let the bastards come in here if they want you, Rosey, but don't you, so help me, move outside this room. It was four o'clock in the morning then, and if we'd have raised the blinds we'd have seen daylight.

NICK: Did he go?

MEYER: Sure he went! He turned around in the door and says — "Don't let the waiter take away my coffee," then he stepped out onto the sidewalk and they shot him three times in his full belly, and drove away.

GATSBY *(to Nick)*:   They electrocuted four of them.

MEYER: Five, with Booker.

(He smiles at Nick)

I understand you are looking for a business connection?

GATSBY *(sharply)*:   No! This isn't the man.

MEYER: But I thought —

GATSBY: No — Mr. Carraway is just a friend.

MEYER: I beg your pardon, I had a wrong man.

(There is the sound of talk and laughter from off stage right on the veranda. Gatsby looks)

GATSBY: The crowd is gathering.

MEYER: Ain't it wonderful! Two or three nights a week maybe! Such a crowd, such fine people. Nobody needs no invitation to come to Mr. Gatsby's, all they need is an automobile, borrowed maybe. Sometimes they just come here and eat and drink and just go. They don't even know which one is Mr. Gatsby! Just real pleasure, nothing formal.

(Catherine, a chorus girl, comes in at the back with a crowd. In the crowd are Doc Civet, Gay, Turner, and three girls. A Footman moves among them with wine. There is ad lib talk and laughter and Catherine sees Meyer and comes to the window)

CATHERINE: Meyer! Well I'll be damned!

MEYER: It's mutual!

Party scene in Gatsby's library, with women in bathing attire.

DOC CIVET: Hello there, old boy. Come on out and have a drink.

CATHERINE: Here's a swell chance for you to be a cut-up, Meyer, all the drinks are on the house.

MEYER: All right, I'm coming.

(Meyer exits to crowd, leaving Gatsby alone with Nick. In a moment the crowd move off)

NICK: What he says is true, I suppose, about the crowd who come here to your parties.

GATSBY: Why yes, old man, true enough.

NICK: But why do you stand for it?

GATSBY: Why not?

NICK: To entertain God knows who!

GATSBY: To keep open house! That's one of the phrases I always liked the sound of, but I had another reason.

NICK: I don't get it.

GATSBY: If all Long Island came drifting through these rooms of mine, I knew that sooner or later she would come, just as she is coming tonight.

NICK: Look here, Gatsby! You are speaking about my cousin.

GATSBY: Yes.

NICK: It isn't exactly the usual thing, you know, to talk about a married woman as —

GATSBY *(breaks in)*:   This isn't a usual thing, Mr. Carraway. I am not in the habit just lately of explaining my actions to any man, but I want you to understand.

NICK: Tom Buchanan is the most jealous man I've ever known. You don't want to make any trouble for her?

GATSBY: It is necessary that she and I should meet and have some talks together. It is absolutely necessary! What will come from these talks I don't know, any more than you do. You have a pretty good head on your shoulders, look at me — I think you know that I couldn't ever do anything, so help me God I couldn't, that wasn't the very best thing I could do for her in every way.

(A noisy party of drunken men and girls crowd on at back singing, and Daisy, Tom, and Jordan Baker force their way through the crowd following Ryan and enter room)

RYAN: Mr. and Mrs. Buchanan, Miss Baker.

(He exits)

DAISY *(at window)*:   Hello there.

MRS. GAY *(on balcony, to Jordan)*:   Oh, Miss Baker. Sorry you didn't win today.

JORDAN: Thanks.

MRS. GAY: Don't you remember me? I met you here about a month ago.

JORDAN: Yes, but you've dyed your hair since then. Hello, Mr. Carraway.

(She crosses to him. Tom, on the veranda, has stopped a waiter and takes a drink with a girl in the crowd. Gatsby crosses to Daisy in the window. Jordan crosses in to Nick, and she is followed by Mrs. Gay and Mrs. Turner)

MRS. TURNER: Do you come to these parties often, Miss Baker?

JORDAN: No.

MRS. TURNER: The last one I came to was the one I met you at.

MRS. GAY: Me too.

MRS. TURNER: I like to come. I never care what I do, so I always have a good time.

MRS. GAY: Last time I was here I tore my gown on a chair and he asked me my name and address, Mr. Gatsby did, and inside a week I got a box from Croirier's with a new evening gown in it!

JORDAN: And of course you kept it?

MRS. GAY: I'll give you three guesses!

MRS. TURNER: I told my husband there was something funny about a man who would do a thing like that. He doesn't want any trouble with anybody.

NICK: Who doesn't?

MRS. TURNER: Gatsby!

MRS. GAY: Who is he? Does anybody know?

JORDAN: He's just a man named Gatsby.

MRS. TURNER: He's a bootlegger of course, child, and one time he killed a man who found out he was a nephew to Von Hindenburg and second cousin to the devil! Come on! The boys will be getting soused without us if we don't look out.

MRS. GAY: There's Milt talking to that dirty little Walker girl. Wait till I tell him a few!

(Mrs. Gay and Mrs. Turner exit to veranda as Gatsby and Daisy enter room)

DAISY *(to Nick)*: Oh, Nick! A party like this excites me so! If you want to kiss me anytime during the evening just let me know and I'll be glad to arrange it. Just mention my name, or present a green card.

(Tom enters)

Oh, Tom!

TOM: Well?

DAISY: This is Mr. Gatsby.

TOM: Oh! How are you?

(They shake hands)

My wife tells me she used to know you years ago.

GATSBY: Yes.

TOM: I've heard about you and these parties of yours, queer thing her knowing you — well — I think I'll roam about a bit and look the crowd over.

DAISY: Yes, do, go ahead and if you want to take down any addresses I'll lend you my little gold pencil.

TOM: Oh, I guess I can manage to take care of myself.

(He exits to veranda and joins a group and presently all exit)

DAISY: I never in all my life saw so many celebrities! There is the cunningest little movie star out there with wonderful red hair — and she's drunk.

JORDAN: She's worse when she isn't.

GATSBY *(at arch stage left)*:   I am going to show Mrs. Buchanan my pictures. Would you care to see them?

DAISY: No you wouldn't. Mr. Gatsby and I are going to look at them all by ourselves; you two are going to sit out here and whistle in case of fire, riot or any act of God.

JORDAN: Tom has had two or three too many drinks, you know. You don't want a row.

DAISY: Of course I do! It's all your fault, Nick, you gave me two too many drinks yourself.

GATSBY: We will be in the gallery if you want us. Come, Mrs. Buchanan.

DAISY: Daisy is my name, you know, to my friends.

GATSBY: Come, Daisy.

(Gatsby and Daisy exit stage left)

NICK: I can't make him out, but for some reason I like the man.

JORDAN: He represents everything you hate.

NICK: But there is something gorgeous about the chap. Have you watched him? He reminds me of one of those intricate machines that register earthquakes ten thousand miles away. He has the damnedest gift for hope, for belief in himself and anybody he wants to believe in! Where is he from and what does he do? Does anybody know?

JORDAN: He told me once he was an Oxford man.

NICK: I heard that.

JORDAN: However, I don't believe it.

NICK: Why not?

JORDAN: I don't know. I just don't think he went there.

NICK: No — I'm afraid not.

JORDAN: Anyhow he gives large parties, and I like large parties, they're so intimate. At small parties there isn't any privacy.

NICK: I'm a bit worried. This Gatsby is mad about Daisy.

JORDAN: I don't know as I'd worry. Daisy can take care of herself pretty well, thank you.

NICK: If ever she cared about this fellow she had forgotten it when she married Tom.

JORDAN: She hasn't such a very good memory, you know. I saw them at Santa Barbara when they were on their honeymoon. My dear man, it was awful! She used to sit on the sand with his head in her lap by the hour. I never saw a girl so mad about her husband.

NICK: Then it's all right.

JORDAN: That was in August, a week after I left Santa Barbara Tom ran into a wagon on the Ventura road one night and ripped a front wheel off his car. The girl who was with him got into the papers too, because her arm was broken. She was one of the chambermaids in the Santa Barbara hotel.

NICK: Tough on Daisy.

JORDAN: Yes, and there was another scandal just before her baby was born — but she's been fine. They go about with a wild bunch, but she's kept a perfectly spotless reputation. I guess it's because she's never gone in for amour at all, yet there is something in that voice of hers — if she ever so much as looks over the edge she'll go all the way down.

(Dance music outside)

Oh! They're beginning to dance.

(She rises)

Come on!

NICK: All right.

(As they turn to go, Myrtle Wilson, a young woman of about twenty-two enters on veranda, stage left, looking anxiously and eagerly toward the dancing outside at stage right. Myrtle is dressed simply. She is the wife of Wilson the chauffeur and is sulky and defiant. As Nick and Jordan turn upstage Jordan and Myrtle meet in the open window)

JORDAN: Oh, I know you.

MYRTLE *(defiant)*: Well?

JORDAN: You're the chauffeur's wife, Wilson's.

MYRTLE: And you got him fired from a good job to work in this hippodrome, didn't you? You and that Mrs. Buchanan! I'd like to know why you did it, but I know too much about you to ask you the reason.

JORDAN: About me?

MYRTLE: Oh, a chauffeur hears quite a lot besides the cop that bawls him out!

NICK: Come on, let's dance!

MYRTLE *(as they go)*: You two women cost him a good job, and you made trouble for me.

JORDAN: Servants' quarters in the rear. Come along!

(Dance music is going on — one or two couples dance as far on stage center as to be in sight. Nick puts his arm about Jordan and they dance out at stage right. Myrtle stands in window looking wistfully at the dancers. Catherine and Doc Civet dance on — Doc is drunk and has trouble staying on his feet. Catherine pushes him away)

CATHERINE: Oh, good Lord! Are you all feet?

DOC CIVET: What's matter?

CATHERINE: You're all right, Doc, both of us, go get a drink, you look thirsty!

(She sees Myrtle)

Hello! Myrtle Carey! I thought you'd moved out to Woodlawn or somewhere.

DOC CIVET: Introduce me your friend.

CATHERINE: Go chase yourself. See if you can't find you a wife or some little thing like that.

DOC CIVET: That's all right about findin' a wife. I can find lots of them and it don't make a damn bit of difference to me whose wife I find.

(He exits)

CATHERINE: Well, Myrtle! I haven't seen you since you left the show. Two years ago wasn't it?

MYRTLE: I been married two years.

CATHERINE: To Buck Wilson. Is he fighting now or driving a car?

MYRTLE: He's chauffeur here for Mr. Gatsby. We've only been here a few days.

CATHERINE: I always said you'd marry him. I never knew a girl with pretty legs yet that had any brains.

MYRTLE *(bitterly)*: You don't need either pretty legs or brains in my job. Brains! I didn't even have enough to work in a chorus.

CATHERINE *(sits)*: Wake up already?

MYRTLE: Brains! I was crazy when I married him. Just crazy. I knew right away I'd made a mistake. He borrowed somebody's best suit to get married in, and never even told me about it; and the man came in to get it one day when he was out. "Oh, is this your suit?" I said. "This is the first I ever heard about it." But I gave it to him, then I lay down and cried to beat the band all afternoon.

CATHERINE: Forget him dear. Can him and find yourself a nice sweetie.

MYRTLE: Oh, I wouldn't do anything like that.

CATHERINE: Oh, I don't know. Ned Wicks told me he saw you down at Beefsteak Charlie's with a great big good looking feller only two weeks ago. He knew him too, said he used to be a famous Yale football player named Tom Buchanan.

MYRTLE: Tell Ned Wicks to keep his damn mouth shut, same as I used to tell him. Ask him how much he's charging now for introducing guys with big pocket books and bigger bellies to some "nice little girl that don't object to a good time."

CATHERINE: Well he just happened to mention it.

MYRTLE: If he "just happen to mention it" to Buck he'd have got himself aplenty of trouble and me too.

CATHERINE: Well, suppose you did kick out a little just once? A girl can't live forever.

(Wilson enters at back looking about; he is in his chauffeur's livery. He sees Myrtle and steps into open window)

WILSON: I been looking for you.

CATHERINE *(startled)*: Oh!

(Both girls turn)

WILSON: Come on.

MYRTLE: This is Catherine Carey, Buck; she was in the show with me.*

WILSON *(sternly)*: You've no business here.

* Myrtle Wilson and Catherine Carey appear to be sisters, as in the novel. Both have the surname "Carey." (See p. 55.) Buck, who is married to Myrtle, should know this. Perhaps the problem was ironed out in performance.

CATHERINE: Who has? God knows nobody asked <u>me</u>! My friend and me was with a couple of prunes that didn't have the price of a drink so we turned in here.

WILSON: Come back to the cottage.

MYRTLE: And sit and look at you read the sporting news! You're dumb, Buck. You're so damned dumb you don't know you're alive.

CATHERINE: That's my cue. I just love happy married couples. But all I've got is my face and I always duck out just before the dishes start to fly.

(She exits)

MYRTLE *(to Wilson)*:   The first one of the old gang I've seen for six months. You would have to shame me.

WILSON: There's something wrong, Myrtle. I don't know what it is, but I'm going to know. You are trying to put something over on me, if I find out it's what I think it is, there is going to be hell!

(Ryan comes to window)

RYAN: Wilson!

WILSON: Well?

RYAN: Take the roadster and deliver a message to Mr. Raymond.

WILSON: Now?

RYAN: Yes, it's a small suitcase, I'll get it for you, and tell your wife she has no business here.

WILSON: Go to White Plains this time of night?

RYAN: Why not? You can make it and back in five hours.

WILSON: Out all night again. This is a hell of a job!

RYAN: If you don't like it you know what you can do.

WILSON: I'll go —

(He turns to Myrtle)

Go back to the cottage.

MYRTLE: Yes, Buck.

(She exits)

WILSON: Where's the suitcase?

RYAN: Come with me.

WILSON: What's in these packages I am delivering all over the place? Money?

RYAN: Is that any business of yours?

WILSON: Not if it's all right it ain't any business of mine, but is it all right? I'm no boob, you know, and no fall guy.

RYAN: This isn't a bad job, Wilson, for the right sort of a man, but I wouldn't pull any of that bluster of yours in front of Mr. Gatsby — I've seen fellows that tried it.

(As they turn to go Tom enters)

TOM *(Sees Wilson)*: Oh! So you got that job, didn't you?

WILSON *(sulky)*: Yes, and I don't know why I got it any more than I know why you fired me.

TOM: What's the odds, you're all right now.

WILSON: I hope I am! I hope there's nothing wrong with me or anyone that belongs to me.

(He looks defiantly at Tom and exits through one window as Nick enters through another)

TOM: Hello! Where's Daisy?

NICK: Why?

TOM: She's not out there. What sort of a joint is this anyway? Where the devil did Daisy ever meet this Gatsby? By God, I may be old fashioned in my ideas, but women run around too much these days to suit me. They meet all kinds of crazy fish. Who's he? Some big bootlegger?

NICK: Where did you hear that?

TOM: I didn't hear it. I guessed it. A lot of this new heavy money crowd are just big bootleggers.

NICK: Not Gatsby. He owns a chain of drug stores I think, something like that.

TOM: He looks pretty shady to me. I don't like to have my wife running about with shady people.

NICK: You're crazy, Tom.

TOM: Where is she? Tell me that. I've heard quite a lot about Gatsby around my place this last week, you know! I'd like to know a little about him and I think I'll make it my business to find out. Drug stores! Why should —

(As he speaks Daisy and Gatsby enter through arch at stage left and Tom stops, looking at them)

DAISY: Hello! We have been looking at Mr. Gatsby's pictures.

TOM: I think you'd better come along. This is a little too much of a menagerie to suit me.

DAISY: Lots of people come who haven't been invited. They simply crash their way in and he's too polite to object.

TOM: They're all drunk out there, every one of them.

DAISY: Yes dear, I noticed that as soon as you began to talk.

TOM: I've been looking for you, I tell you.

DAISY: Yes, yes — I know. Forget it and come have a dance. Excuse me, Mr. Gatsby.

GATSBY: I hope you will forgive me if I have taken too much of your time.

DAISY: I loved the pictures. Come on, Tom.

(She crosses to window)

Oh! There are a lot of new people. I am sure there must be one or two pretty girls, Tom, that you haven't had a chance to look over.

(Daisy and Tom exit to veranda and off)

GATSBY *(to Nick)*:   She doesn't like my party.

NICK: Of course she does.

GATSBY: She isn't having a good time.

NICK: What's the trouble?

GATSBY: It isn't the way I thought it would be. I feel far away from her. It's hard to make her understand. It used to be different.

NICK: I wouldn't ask too much of her. You can't repeat the past.

GATSBY: Can't repeat the past! Why, of course you can.

NICK: No.

GATSBY: I am going to fix everything just as it was before.

NICK: She is Buchanan's wife.

GATSBY: I am not thinking about that. She stands for a certain something in my life that I have got to get back again. Only an ideal perhaps, but since I've lost it my life has been all confused and disordered. I've got to go way back and begin again. I thought if I could talk with her it would be all right; now I am afraid.

NICK: It has been seven or eight years, you know.

GATSBY: It may be because I would never let her go. It isn't her fault, she has been as real to me as though she had actually been with me. I suppose I have kept on adding to her image in my brain all these years, decking it out with every bright feather that drifted past me — until that image has become the reality — and she is the dream.

NICK: And she has disappointed you?

GATSBY: She didn't understand, but it must come out all right. Some things are bigger than we are ourselves.

(A few couples dance in at back, among them Daisy and Tom. They stop by the window)

DAISY: My poor husband is all out of condition, Mr. Gatsby. Don't you want to cut in?

GATSBY: Of course I do.

TOM *(angry)*:   Wait a minute.

DAISY: Don't be silly, Tom. Come on.

(Gatsby puts his arm about her and they dance on the veranda. Tom crosses down to Nick)

TOM: Damned queer.

NICK: What is?

TOM: The way Daisy is acting.

NICK: Queer? Got a cigarette?

TOM: Sure. See her dancing with that mountebank!

(He offers cigarette to Nick from a silver case)

NICK: Gatsby?

TOM: Whatever his name is. How much have those two seen of one another this last week?

NICK: I wouldn't make an ass of myself if I were you. I think I'll go out and see what's going on.

(He exits to veranda. Tom crosses to table and pours himself a drink. Outside on the veranda Gatsby and Daisy pass out of sight at stage right. Myrtle enters on the veranda at stage left, looking about. She has changed to an evening dress. She sees Tom through the window and steps quickly in)

MYRTLE: Tom!

TOM *(turns)*:   Hello! I thought you were going to send me word where I could see you.

MYRTLE *(crosses to him)*: I didn't have a chance. Buck has been wild ever since you fired him. For a little while I thought he knew something. He found the door key you gave me to the apartment on Seventy-Second Street in my bag. I tried to stall but I'm afraid I made a mess of it.

TOM: He can't know anything.

MYRTLE: Your wife didn't know anything but she got me out of the house.

TOM: We'll have to be careful.

MYRTLE: Careful! Buck's dangerous, Tom, I tell you you've got to take me away.

TOM: We'll see; when can you meet me in town?

MYRTLE: I wouldn't dare to, but I can see you tonight, Tom. Buck is driving all the way to White Plains, he just started. We've got a little cottage alone, the second one past the garage, you can't miss it. I'll have a light burning and the door open.

TOM: I'll come.

MYRTLE: He might have left some one to watch me. I don't think so but if everything is all right the light will be burning.

(Milton Gay enters quite drunk and crosses gravely to the bookshelves and looks at books — Turner, another guest, crosses to table and takes drink)

TURNER: Pardon me! I know two's company.

TOM *(coldly)*: Not at all.

(Gatsby and Daisy and Nick enter; as Myrtle sees Daisy she turns and exits. Daisy crosses to Tom)

DAISY: Who is that woman?

TOM: Some nut. What are any of them? A bunch of bums!

65

DAISY: Tom! You are insulting to Mr. Gatsby.

TOM: Oh no. If I ever want to get insulting to Mr. Gatsby he'll know it.

GATSBY *(pleasantly)*: I don't see any especial reason why you should be insulting to me, old sport.

TOM: Don't you? That's good. Then of course everything is all right.

DAISY: Nick? Where's Jordan?

NICK: I don't know. I've been looking for her.

(Milton Gay holds up a book he has taken from the bookcase and calls with drunken gravity to Turner)

MILTON: Say, Turner! Say! They're all real.

TURNER: The books?

MILTON: Absolutely real. Have pages and everything! It fooled me all right. Look! A real history. This feller Gatsby is a regular Belasco. What realism. Knew when to stop, too. Didn't cut a page.

TURNER: Oh, he's a wonder, this feller Gatsby!

(He crosses to Gatsby)

Say, friend. Who brought you, or did you just come? I was just brought, most people were brought.

GATSBY: I happen to live here. My name is Gatsby.

TURNER: Say! Milt! He's real! Two legs and everything. Honest to God there is a Gatsby!

(There is the sound of a woman screaming and Mrs. Gay and Mrs. Turner enter. Mrs. Gay is screaming. Mrs. Turner half supports her and Doc Civet follows anxiously)

GAY: Say, what's the matter with my wife?

TURNER: I'm sure I don't know where this man Gatsby gets his booze! It certainly makes her act funny.

MRS. GAY: They wanted to stick my head in the swimming pool and I wouldn't let 'em. Oh! Oh!

MRS. TURNER: It would have been good for you.

MRS. GAY: Anything I hate is to get my head stuck in a pool. They almost drowned me once over in Jersey.

DOC CIVET: Nerves all unstrung, better take her home. I'm a medical man.

MRS. GAY: You are.

DOC CIVET: Yes, I am. Drunk or sober.

GAY: She's all right, when she's had five or six drinks she always acts that way.

DOC CIVET: Then she ought to leave it alone.

MRS. GAY: I do leave it alone.

DOC CIVET: I'm speaking as a medical man.

MRS. GAY: Well, speak for yourself. Your hand shakes. I wouldn't let you operate on me.

(Meyer Wolfshiem, quite sober, enters at back)

MEYER: Oh! Mr. Gatsby! They are going down to the swimming pool. Look at all the bathing beauties.

(Jordan, Catherine, and two or three other girls all in one-piece bathing suits enter at back. Jordan goes to window)

JORDAN: Hello there! We are going to have a swim.

NICK *(shocked)*:   Miss Baker!

TOM: Well, I'll be damned!

JORDAN: I honestly believe the men are shocked!

(Girls laugh)

CATHERINE: Anybody who has a head like mine follow me.

(Exit at stage right Jordan, Catherine and the bathing girls)

NICK: I'll take care of Miss Baker, Tom. Take Daisy to my place. It's getting a little rough here.

DAISY: Yes, I think it's time to go. Good night, Mr. Gatsby.

GATSBY: I'll get a man with a flashlight, you'd better take the short cut across my lawn.

(Tom, Daisy, Gatsby exit at back)

DOC CIVET *(to Meyer)*: Say, I just had the damndest fight with a dame out there that said she was my wife.

MEYER: You got a good reason!

TURNER *(to Mrs. Turner)*: Come on. Behave yourself.

MRS. TURNER: Yes, that's right. Whenever he sees I'm having a good time he wants to go home.

MRS. GAY: Never heard anything so selfish in all my life.

MRS. TURNER: We are always the first ones to leave.

MRS. GAY: So are we.

MILTON: Well, we're about the last tonight. Everybody has gone but those bathers.

TURNER: Come on, now.

MRS. TURNER: No!

TURNER: Like hell you won't.

(He picks her up and runs out with her, followed by Mr. and Mrs. Gay — by now all but Meyer have gone. He lights cigar. Ryan shuts all the windows but the one at center and crosses down to him)

RYAN: That's the last of them except the girls in the pool; some of the boys are waiting to see Mr. Gatsby.

MEYER: It's safe enough I guess to bring them in.

(Gatsby enters)

GATSBY: Ryan, did you hear from Toledo?

RYAN: Yes, Mr. Gatsby, the bank took the bonds all right and paid by certified check.

MEYER: Good.

RYAN: Donnivan is here.

GATSBY: Get him! Then stay on the veranda and keep a look out.

RYAN: Yes, Mr. Gatsby.

(He exits)

MEYER: That's big money from Toledo.

GATSBY: We need every dollar of it and more! It's the Donnivan business that will make us solid. There is three quarters of a million in it.

MEYER: You'll get it. You got luck. I always said so. I remember the first day I seen you I said that.

GATSBY: I know.

MEYER: You was a young major, just out of the war, and covered over with medals. You was so hard up you had to keep on wearing your uniform because you couldn't buy no regular clothes.

GATSBY: I was still groggy from a blow I'd taken, I didn't care much what happened.

MEYER *(smiles)*: You was hungry. I asked you to lunch with me and you ate more than four dollars' worth of food in half an hour.

(Ryan enters, followed by Donnivan, a rough man in shabby clothes. He is not a bum but is quite plainly not a gentleman)

RYAN: Donnivan, sir.

(He steps out on the veranda as Donnivan comes down)

GATSBY: Well?

DONNIVAN: All right, I think, Mr. Gatsby, we are going to try to make a landing tomorrow night.

GATSBY: Where?

DONNIVAN: Below Norfolk. I'm in touch with the ship and everything is ready, the weather reports are in our favor and the boys on shore are all set.

GATSBY: You know what this one means, don't you, Donnivan?

DONNIVAN: I know what it means to me.

GATSBY: That's so.

(He takes a package of yellow backed bills from his pocket)

You know what it means to you! What's the use of my saying anything. Here.

(He counts off ten bills and hands them to Donnivan)

This will take care of everything, don't be afraid to use it.

DONNIVAN: No, Mr. Gatsby. I'll do the best I can.

(During this, on the balcony outside, Crosby, a crook, has entered to Ryan and talked excitedly aside to him. Ryan crosses to window and enters the room, Crosby comes as far forward as the window)

RYAN: Crosby! With bad news, Mr. Gatsby.

MEYER *(alarmed)*: Hello!

GATSBY: In a moment! You all right, Donnivan?

DONNIVAN: Yes, sir.

GATSBY: Good luck then.

DONNIVAN: Thanks.

(He turns and exits)

GATSBY: Well, Crosby?

CROSBY (*comes forward excited*):   This is a hell of a note! Didn't you get my wire?

GATSBY: No.

CROSBY: There's a leak somewhere.

MEYER: What is it? Come on!

CROSBY: Young Park is in trouble. They picked him up when he handed those bonds over the counter. They got a wire from New York giving them the numbers just five minutes before. What do you know about that? You never can tell in these hick towns!

MEYER: The Park boy! He'll talk. I never liked that boy. Always I said —

GATSBY: I'll see him myself tomorrow. Have Sol meet me at the hotel about noon and tell him to have it fixed for us to see him.

CROSBY: Yes, sir.

GATSBY: Get word to the boy that everything will be all right and that he will be looked out for, be around yourself tomorrow, I may want you.

CROSBY: All right. Good night.

(*He exits with Ryan*)

GATSBY: Good night.

(*As Crosby goes*)

MEYER: Right now that's bad. Our first bad break!

GATSBY: It's nothing.

MEYER: Nothing?!

GATSBY (*firmly*):   I won't let it be! Not now.

MEYER: You're just a man, you know. You ain't no god!

GATSBY: Do you see that green light way off there, Meyer ... the little green light on the opposite shore?

MEYER: I see it, yes.

GATSBY: I have come a long way from the hungry boy in his dirty old uniform to this house with its view of that light out there. It has been a dream, all of it, but it is so close now that I know I can really grasp it. This isn't my time to fail!

MEYER: I always did say that a man who gets hunches like you get ought to be a poker player. Well, Mr. Gatsby.

(He rises and looks at his watch)

I ain't so young as I was, and it ain't so early as it might be.

GATSBY *(steps to window and calls)*:   Ryan!

(He turns back)

Go to bed, Meyer. I expect reports from one or two more of our people before I turn in.

RYAN *(enters)*:   Yes, sir.

GATSBY: Mr. Wolfshiem is ready, Ryan.

RYAN: Yes, sir.

MEYER: Good night; get some sleep, everybody has to sleep.

GATSBY: I'm all right. Good night.

(Ryan and Meyer exit through arch. A footman comes on veranda and puts out the veranda lights and the lights of the colored lanterns; he enters room and throws off the switch, leaving only the table light and the moonlight at the open French windows at center. Gatsby has lit a cigar or cigarette)

FOOTMAN: Good night, sir.

GATSBY: Good night.

(The footman exits. Gatsby goes up to window and for a moment looks off at the little green light on the distant shore. As he turns back Daisy runs in to open window of balcony)

DAISY: Jay!

GATSBY *(turns)*: Is something wrong?

DAISY: I've come to you!

GATSBY: I don't understand.

DAISY: Must you understand any more than that?

GATSBY: Yes.

DAISY: You love me! Isn't that enough?

GATSBY: Just half enough.

DAISY: I don't want to be made a fool of! Tom has gone to that woman. He's in with her now. I followed him to her cottage. I saw them meet.

(She enters and crosses to him)

Well! Here I am. Do you want me to stay?

GATSBY *(quietly)*: No.

DAISY: You don't mean that!

GATSBY: I want the thing you promised me, openly, before all the world, and I am going to have it.

DAISY: I am afraid of divorce! I don't like it; I told you that this afternoon. Besides, I am not sure about you. How can I be! You can't bargain with me! I've come to you. If you don't want me, I'll go.

(She starts)

GATSBY: Daisy!

DAISY: How do we know about the future? What do we care? You love me — and I am here!

GATSBY: Not as I want you to be here!

DAISY: You fool! Don't you know if you let me go now you'll never see me again?

73

(As she speaks Jordan and Nick pass at the back. Jordan has on a bathrobe over her evening gown)

JORDAN: Hello! That you, Daisy?

(She stands at window with Nick looking into the dimly lighted room)

GATSBY: Yes, Mrs. Buchanan has been waiting here for you; it's late, you had better take her home.

CURTAIN

ACT III

SCENE

The same set.

It is a very hot afternoon about ten days later. The sun beats down fiercely but on the veranda outside the sun curtains are lowered. Ryan is at telephone. Meyer, his coat off, and a palm leaf fan in his hand, sits bending eagerly forward, listening to Ryan. On the table beside Meyer is a long cool drink.

MEYER *(eagerly)*: Well? Is it?

RYAN: They don't answer.

MEYER: Try! Keep on trying!

RYAN: It's no use.

   (He puts the phone down)

MEYER *(gravely)*: Nobody answering from there means trouble.

RYAN: Mr. Gatsby will know. He was going there himself.

MEYER: I don't know. Things ain't so good these last few days. There's something working hard against Mr. Gatsby — maybe his luck has gone.

RYAN *(bitterly)*: It's this married woman! He never bothered with women any more than to kid along with them. Now look at him.

MEYER: He works hard enough, too hard maybe, but I don't know; he ain't like the same man at all.

RYAN: He's nervous, of course, about Donnivan.

MEYER: "No news might be good news," how do we know? Don't make me worry on such a hot day! Maybe you think I ought to sweat hot and cold at the same time.

(He sits back in his chair fanning himself as Tom Buchanan enters at back on veranda and comes to the window)

TOM: Mr. Gatsby here?

RYAN: No sir, Mr. Gatsby went to town very early. He expected to be back by this time. Any message, sir?

TOM: No. I'll have a word with this gentleman, Mr. —

MEYER *(coldly)*: Wolfshiem.

TOM: Yes, then I'll run along.

RYAN: Yes, sir.

(He exits arch stage left)

TOM: Hot, isn't it?

MEYER: It's terrible.

(Fans himself)

TOM: You're a friend of Mr. Gatsby's?

MEYER: Yes, I am.

TOM: I am told it was you who started him in business.

MEYER: Started him! I made him!

TOM: Oh.

MEYER: I raised him up out of nothing, right out of the gutter! I saw right away he was a fine appearing gentlemanly young man, and I knew I could use him good. I got him to join up in the American Legion and right away he did some work for me in Albany. We were like brothers almost, in no time.

TOM: And you are in business with him now?

MEYER *(draws away)*: Me? Oh, no, sir. I'm retired.

TOM: You're a gambler, aren't you?

MEYER: No!

TOM: Yes, you.

MEYER: I ain't so young, Mr. Buchanan, and I got a little money put away and so I just sit around, and play a little golf maybe and in the winter time maybe take a little run down to Palm Beach, that's all.

TOM: And so you deny having any business connection at all with Mr. Gatsby?

MEYER *(rises)*: I say they ain't no man alive got a piece of paper to prove that I got any business connections at all with anybody.

TOM: Oh. You play them safe.

MEYER: Maybe it's cooler up in my room. I'm going there.

TOM: If I were you I would go further than that room, Mr. Wolfshiem. You know what the rats do, don't you, when the ship is sinking?

MEYER: It's pretty hot ain't it to talk like a damn fool — maybe I'll take a little bath. I might get cooler.

(He exits through arch. Tom looks about for a moment, then turns to go as Wilson enters at back. Wilson looks wild-eyed and distressed)

WILSON: I was looking for Mr. Gatsby.

TOM: He's out, I believe.

(He starts)

WILSON *(firmly)*: Wait!

TOM: What do you mean?

WILSON: You know that old car of mine, the one I used to drive nights when you didn't want me?

TOM: Well?

WILSON: I was hoping that either you or Mr. Gatsby would give me something for it. I need money pretty bad.

TOM: I don't want it.

WILSON: It's all right for a servant's car, and you could have it cheap.

TOM: What do you want money for all of a sudden?

WILSON: I've been here too long. I want to get away. I want to take my wife away, Mr. Buchanan.

TOM: Oh!

WILSON: I got wised up to something funny about ten days ago, that's why I want to get away.

TOM: Well, ask Gatsby! I don't want your car.

(He starts)

WILSON: Hold on!

(He catches Tom's hand)

TOM: Take your hand off me.

WILSON: You listen, and don't try any of your college football stuff on me, or I'll hand you something big as you are!

TOM: What do you want?

WILSON: I want to know what's wrong with my wife. I want to know who it is that's been setting her against me.

TOM: Why don't you ask her, or have you frightened her away?

WILSON: I've got her locked up in my cottage there. I'm going to keep her locked up until I know who the man is that's taken her away from me.

TOM: What business is it of mine?

WILSON: I think you're the man!

TOM: You're crazy!

WILSON: That's what she says. She won't tell me the truth.

TOM: Why should you think that I —

WILSON: It began early this summer when I was working for
you. She's treated me like dirt since then — I watched her, but
I didn't see anything, but there was something funny in the
way you fired me that day.

TOM: I didn't need two men.

WILSON: You've been here since we have, two or three times.

TOM: What of it?

WILSON: I was out on an errand until morning on Wednesday.
Some man was there with her in my cottage all that night.

TOM: Pretty raw thing to say about your own wife, Wilson!

WILSON: See that?

(Takes a silver cigarette case out of his pocket and holds it out)

Is that yours?

TOM: No, no! Of course it isn't mine.

WILSON: When I left at ten it wasn't there and she'd gone to
bed. She was still in bed when I got in next morning, and I saw
this, on the floor back of a chair.

TOM: Why didn't you ask her to explain —

WILSON: Because she's explained too much. I'm going to do
the explaining now. It won't be so hard to find out who owns
this thing.

TOM: Who sent you out on that errand that kept you out all
night?

WILSON: Mr. Gatsby. Why?

TOM: He's sent you away three or four nights lately.

WILSON: Yes —

TOM: I am going now, Wilson. If I were you I wouldn't look for trouble.

WILSON: What do you mean?

TOM: He's a strong man, Gatsby.

WILSON: Mr. Buchanan ...

TOM: Better return his cigarette box. He won't like your keeping it.

WILSON: Yes, by God, I'll return it!

TOM: Now don't be a fool!

WILSON: I've got to see her. I have got to be sure.

TOM: Steady now.

WILSON: I have got to be sure.

(Wilson exits. Tom looks after him as Ryan enters)

RYAN: Mr. Gatsby has returned, sir. He is changing.

TOM: I'll drop in later. My wife and I drove over to spend the afternoon with Mr. Carraway. Warm, isn't it?

RYAN: Very warm, sir.

(As Tom exits, Meyer enters through arch)

MEYER: He's gone, that Mr. Buchanan?

RYAN: Yes.

MEYER: He means trouble. I don't know what, but I can always tell!

(Gatsby enters through arch)

GATSBY: I'm late.

MEYER: That don't matter, is it good news or bad?

GATSBY: I can't get any word from Donnivan.

MEYER: Well, I don't know — "no news may be good news."

GATSBY: There's some trouble with the bank. I can't understand it. They have called in that twenty thousand loan on me.

MEYER: Did you pay it?

GATSBY: Yes, I had to pay it, but I don't understand, and they wouldn't give me a reason.

MEYER: It ain't so good when a bank does that.

GATSBY: Someone has been talking, but it's all right, if the Donnivan deal is safe, we can laugh at all of them.

MEYER: And if it ain't?

GATSBY: It must be right!

RYAN: Crosby is here, sir. He seems worried.

GATSBY: Bring him in.

(Ryan exits at arch)

The Park boy was in court today. That case looks bad, but he swore to me he would keep quiet.

MEYER: He's got a bad face, that boy. I never liked him.

CROSBY: They held the boy, Mr. Gatsby, for the grand jury!

GATSBY: All right. We had to expect that, but we can get him off at his trial. I'll take charge of it myself.

CROSBY: There won't be any trial, Mr. Gatsby.

MEYER: What?!

CROSBY: The boy is going to take a suspended sentence and turn state's evidence.

RYAN: Then they've got the whole of us!

GATSBY *(sternly)*:   That's enough, Ryan.

RYAN: I beg your pardon, Mr. Gatsby.

GATSBY: We can beat this thing! It may cost money, but we can do it.

MEYER: If you got the money.

GATSBY: Why do you say "you" — you said "us" a little while ago.

MEYER: If I like a business I get in it, if I don't like it I get out.

(Footman enters through arch)

FOOTMAN: Mr. Donnivan.

(The footman steps aside as Donnivan enters; then the footman exits)

DONNIVAN: Is it all right here?

GATSBY: Go on.

DONNIVAN: They got us!

GATSBY: Oh — got us?

MEYER: So.

RYAN: That settles it.

DONNIVAN: We stood off shore for three days because there was a moon, and we had a hot tip they were looking for us. Night before last I took a chance and started in a small boat to look the ground over. I hadn't got halfway to shore when I heard a machine gun going. I turned back until I saw a cutter right alongside of us and the uniforms on our deck. They took her into Norfolk yesterday.

(He looks from one to another of the three men who stand silent)

Gentlemen! I did the best I could, you know what it meant to me.

GATSBY: Yes, no one blames you, old sport. It's a bad thing for all of us.

DONNIVAN: It was my chance and I missed it. I won't get another. You know where to find me, Mr. Gatsby.

GATSBY: All right, Donnivan.

DONNIVAN: If we'd got the stuff through it would have made us rich. Hell!

(He exits with Ryan)

MEYER: Well, Mr. Gatsby, I don't like to go out in the sun on such a hot day, but I must be starting.

GATSBY: Where?

MEYER: To New York first, then tonight maybe to Schroon Lake to play a little golf with some friends of mine.

GATSBY: Just what do you mean, Meyer? Let's put the cards on the table.

MEYER: They've smashed you up, Gatsby. I got to get out. I can't get mixed up in it. When a man gets smashed I never like to get mixed up in it. When I was a young man it was different, if a friend of mine got into trouble I'd stick to him to the end. I can't do it now. I got to be careful.

(Ryan enters)

GATSBY: Order Mr. Wolfshiem's car, he is leaving.

RYAN: So am I.

GATSBY: You too, Ryan?

(The other servants, two cooks, two footmen, three maids and two outside men enter through the arch and stand in a sulky group)

RYAN: All of them are going, Mr. Gatsby. They say there have been detectives watching this place for the last three days. They are afraid of trouble.

GATSBY: But it was you who told them it was time to go.

RYAN: Yes, I told 'em that.

GATSBY: Then you go! Now!

(He turns to the crowd of servants)

You can go tonight, all of you, if you want to, but I expect company this afternoon and I am going to ask you to remain at least until my guests have gone.

PARLOR MAID *(to French cook)*:   Tell him, Adolph.

COOK: Now! Now!

RYAN: It's no good, they won't stay.

GATSBY: Very well.

(He takes money out of pocket and gives it to Ryan)

I think this will pay them all in full. If there is anything over, divide it between them.

MEYER: Maybe you'd better go yourself, while you can.

GATSBY: No.

MEYER: Everybody knows his own business best, anyhow I hope you know yours. Well, so long, Mr. Gatsby.

(Meyer, Ryan and the servants exit at stage left through arch. Gatsby is left alone. He crosses to safe and opens it and takes out a tin dispatch box and unlocks the box and takes out some papers. As he does so he draws out by accident an old copy book and it falls on table. Gatsby selects the papers he wants, and locks the box, and turns away, leaving the old copy book on the table. On the veranda outside is heard a woman's laugh and Daisy comes on and crosses to the window, followed by Nick and Jordan)

DAISY: Is it cool in here? If it isn't we won't come in.

JORDAN: Don't be silly. It isn't cool anywhere. Oh, Lord! What a day!

DAISY: It's cooler than your stuffy little place anyway, Nick.

(She crosses and gives her hand to Gatsby)

I told you last night I'd come. You see I kept my word.

GATSBY: I knew you would. Sit here, there's a little air, and here's a fan.

DAISY: You're a darling!

(She turns suddenly and throws her arms about his neck and kisses him)

You know I love you!

JORDAN: You forget there's a lady present.

DAISY: That's all right. You kiss Nick too.

JORDAN: What a low, vulgar girl.

DAISY: I don't care!

(Starts to dance gaily about the room)

NICK: You're crazy! Sit down, you make me hotter just to look at you.

DAISY *(sits)*:   Oh dear! What'll we do with ourselves this afternoon and the day after that, and the next thirty years?

JORDAN: Don't be morbid. Life starts all over again when it gets crisp in the fall.

DAISY: I don't see why I shouldn't have a drink, a nice long cool drink.

JORDAN: That's it. Ring for a drink, Mr. Gatsby.

GATSBY: Of course.

(He turns to push the button, then suddenly remembers that all the servants have left)

I'll have to ask you to excuse me for a moment.

(He crosses toward arch)

DAISY: What's the matter? Why don't you sit down and behave?

GATSBY: I want to see about your drink myself. I have a great idea.

(He exits)

JORDAN: Tom is around, you know, Daisy. Suppose he had seen you just now … when you kissed Gatsby?

DAISY: Suppose every wife in the world had seen you every time one of their husbands kissed you — don't be a frog! Croak! Croak! Croak! If it comes right down to kissing, Tom isn't so bad at it himself.

NICK: You're careless people, Daisy, you and Tom. You have a way of smashing up things and creatures, then retreating back into your money, or your vast carelessness, or whatever the tie is that keeps you together, and you leave other people to clean up the mess you have made.

DAISY: Nick! You're as smug as the devil at his damndest and oily as a fish!

(She rises)

I hate you very much, and I think I'll go home.

(She crosses and her eyes fall on the small account book that Gatsby dropped on the desk)

Hello!

(She picks it up)

It looks like a little boy's exercise book.

(She opens it)

J. Gatsby! That's funny, J. Gatsby. The last two letters have been written in at a different time — it looks like J. Gatz — changed into J. Gatsby. Why, it's a sort of diary.

NICK: Put it down. What business is it of yours?

DAISY: My dear Nick, I want to be vulgar, even the very finest lady has to be vulgar when it's hot.

NICK: He might not want —

DAISY: Hush! Listen. "Sept. 10, 1906 — Schedule: Rise from bed 6 am. Dumbbell exercise and wall scaling 6:15 to 6:30. Study electricity 7:15 to 8:15. Work 8:30 to 4:30 pm. Baseball and sports 4:30 to 5. Practice elocution, poise and how to attain it, 5:00 to 6:00. Study needed inventions 7:00 to 8:00."

JORDAN: Some day!

DAISY *(reads)*: "General Resolves — no time wasted at..." at something, I can't read the word. "No more smoking or chewing. Bath every other day. Read one improving book or magazine a week. Save five dollars" no — "save three dollars per week. Be better to parents."

JORDAN: Poor kid!

DAISY: September, 1906.

JORDAN: He was about eleven, wasn't he?

DAISY *(laughs)*: It just shows you.

NICK: Poor kid. He wanted to get to the top, didn't he?

DAISY: I remember once he told me something about the cement blocks of the pavement in the moonlight making a ladder for him, to take him up to the stars, or above the trees or somewhere, all bunk of course, but it made a terrible hit with me at the time.

JORDAN: That ladder is going to fall over on you two, you know, if you aren't careful.

DAISY: All right, let it fall. I have been just bored to death for the last two years, and I don't care what happens.

(Gatsby enters through the arch with a large tray on which there are glasses, a bowl of ice, a bottle of whiskey and a glass

of mint leaves. Beside this there are four other glasses in each of which there is a mint julep already mixed)

JORDAN: Ah! How did you guess it?

DAISY: But why should you carry that big tray in all by yourself?

GATSBY: Why not? I've carried heavier things.

(He hands the glasses around)

DAISY: Mint julep! Who cares how hot it is.

(As they drink, Tom enters at back along the veranda and into the room)

TOM: Hello.

GATSBY: Come in and have a drink.

TOM: It's too damned hot. What's all that crowd I just saw leaving your side door in the station car?

GATSBY: Some of the servants are going to a party. Why?

TOM: I just wondered. I don't see why we had to ride over here in all this heat, Daisy. We'd be better off at home.

DAISY: We can't move, can we, Jordan?

GATSBY: Do have a little drink, old sport.

DAISY *(coldly)*:   Oh, Tom, you do look so hot, and your face is red. You're right. We can't stand this; let's go to town!

(She rises)

Let's the whole crowd of us go to town.

JORDAN: Good Lord! Why?

TOM: Why not? If she wants to go to town let's go.

JORDAN: Are we just going to rush off like this? Aren't we even going to finish our drinks?

TOM: Come on! What's the matter, anyhow? If we're going to town, let's start.

DAISY: Oh, let's have fun! It's too hot to fuss.

GATSBY: Everybody is going to do just what you want.

DAISY: Thanks.

(She looks up at him boldly as Tom looks on)

You're sweet to me, and you look so nice and cool. You always look so cool.

TOM *(angrily)*:   After all, why should we go to town? Women get these fool notions into their heads.

DAISY: We'd better take something to drink. Ring for a bottle of Scotch, Mr. Gatsby.

GATSBY: I'll get it.

(He crosses)

I won't be long.

(He exits into hall)

TOM *(looks after him)*:   I am just giving him rope, you know, just rope enough to hang himself!

NICK: What?

TOM: You all think I'm pretty dumb, don't you? Perhaps I am, but I have a — almost a second sight sometimes, that tells me what to do. I've made a little investigation of this Gatsby!

DAISY: I suppose you've been to a medium.

TOM: No, I've been looking him up, that's all.

JORDAN: And you found out nothing worse about him than that he was an Oxford man.

TOM: Oxford man! Like hell he is!

JORDAN: But he told me he was.

TOM: Oxford, New Mexico.

DAISY: Listen, Tom — if you're such a snob why are you here?

To m: It's because you are. And you are here I suppose because you used to know this fellow before we were married, God knows where.

(Gatsby enters with a full bottle of Scotch)

Gatsby: Are we ready?

Daisy: No! I'm not going!

Tom: What?

Daisy: I'm going to stay here.

(She sits)

Jordan: Good!

(She sits)

Tom: Well I'll be damned!

Daisy: Even then you won't be any hotter than I am right now. Won't someone please open another window?

Jordan: There aren't any more.

Daisy: Mr. Gatsby could send for an axe.

Tom: The only thing to do is forget about the heat. You make it ten times worse by crabbing about it.

Gatsby: Well, it is pretty hot, you know, old sport.

Tom: That's a great expression of yours, isn't it?

Gatsby: What is?

Tom: All this old sport business! Where'd you pick it up?

Daisy *(rises hastily)*: Now see here, Tom, if you are going to make personal remarks I won't stay for a minute.

Jordan: I think after all we'd better go up to town, we could be in time for May Foster's wedding at the Plaza.

Daisy: Just imagine marrying anyone in this heat. No!

(She sits)

Let's just stay here and behave ourselves.

JORDAN: It is a pretty terrible day to get married.

DAISY: Still, I was married in the middle of June. Louisville in June! I remember somebody fainted. Who was it fainted, Tom?

TOM: A man named Biloxi. "Blocks" Biloxi, and he made boxes, that's a fact, and he was from Biloxi, Tennessee.

JORDAN: They carried him into my house, after he fainted, because we lived just two doors from the church, and he stayed three weeks, until Daddy put him out. The day after he left Daddy died. There wasn't any connection.

NICK: I used to know a Bill Biloxi from Memphis. Remember him, Tom?

TOM: No.

DAISY: Of course you do! He told me he was president of your class at Yale.

TOM: Biloxi?

DAISY: Yes.

NICK: Oh, no.

TOM: By the way, Mr. Gatsby, I understand you are an Oxford man?

GATSBY: Yes, I went there.

TOM: You must have gone there about the time Biloxi went to New Haven.

DAISY: Tom!

(She rises)

GATSBY: I told you I went there.

TOM: I heard you, but I'd like to know when!

GATSBY: It was in 1919. I only stayed five months, that's why I can't really call myself an Oxford man. It was an opportunity they gave to some of the officers after the Armistice. We could go to any of the universities in England, or France.

NICK *(happy)*:   Good boy, Gatsby!

DAISY: Now I am going to make you a drink, Tom, then you won't seem quite so stupid to yourself. Look at the mint.

(She starts to mix drink)

TOM: Wait a minute. I want to ask Mr. Gatsby one more question.

GATSBY: Go on.

DAISY: No!

GATSBY: He wants to come out in the open — well, so do I!

TOM: What kind of a row are you trying to cause in my family anyhow?

DAISY: He isn't causing a row. You're causing a row. Please have a little self-control.

TOM: Self-control! I suppose the latest thing is to sit back and let Mr. Nobody from Nowhere make love to your wife. Well, if that's the idea you can count me out. Nowadays people begin by sneering at family life and family institutions, and next they'll throw everything overboard and have intermarriage between black and white.

JORDAN: We're all white here.

TOM: I know I'm not very popular. I don't give big parties. I suppose you've got to turn your house into a pigsty to have any friends.

NICK: Wait a minute, Tom!

GATSBY: No! I've got something to tell <u>him</u>, old sport.

DAISY: Please don't! Please let's go home, Tom. Why don't we all go home?

TOM: I want to know what Mr. Gatsby has to tell me.

GATSBY: Your wife doesn't love you — she never loved you, she loves me!

TOM: The hell she does.

GATSBY: She loves me.

TOM: You're crazy!

GATSBY: She never loved you. Do you hear? She only married you because I was poor and she was tired of waiting for me. It was a terrible mistake, but in her heart she has never loved anybody but me.

TOM: What's been going on, Daisy? I want to hear all about it.

GATSBY: I told you what's been going on.

JORDAN *(rises)*: Take me out of this, Nick.

GATSBY: No, you stay!

(He turns to Tom)

It's been going on for years, and you never knew.

TOM: Daisy! You've been seeing this fellow for years?

GATSBY: Not seeing. No, we couldn't meet — but both of us loved each other all the time, old sport, and you didn't know. I used to laugh sometimes.

TOM: Oh — that's all. You're crazy! What do I care about what you were fool enough to imagine before I even met Daisy? Only I'm damned if I can figure out how you ever got within a mile of her, unless you brought the groceries to the back door. But all the rest of that's a God-damned lie! Daisy loved me when she married me, and she loves me now.

GATSBY: No!

TOM: She does! The trouble is that sometimes she gets foolish ideas in her head, and doesn't know what she's doing.

GATSBY: After this she'll know what she's doing.

Tom: And I love you too, Daisy. Once in a while I go off on a spree and make a fool of myself, but I always come back, and in my heart I love you all the time.

Daisy: You're revolting! Do you know why we left Louisville, Nick? I'm surprised that nobody has ever treated you to the details of that little spree.

Gatsby: Daisy, that's all over now. It doesn't matter any more. Just tell him the truth, that you never loved him, and it's all wiped out forever.

Daisy (looks at him — Tom):

Why — how could I love him — possibly!

Gatsby: You never loved him.

Daisy: I never loved him.

Tom: Not at Kapiolani?

Daisy: No.

Tom: Not that day I carried you down from the Punch Bowl to keep your shoes dry? Daisy?

Daisy: Please don't!

(She turns on Gatsby)

Oh, you want too much! I love you now, isn't that enough? I can't help what's past. I did love him once, but I love you too.

Gatsby: You love me too?

Tom: Even that's a lie! She didn't know you were alive. Why, there are things between Daisy and me that you'll never know, things that neither of us can ever forget.

Gatsby: I want to speak to you alone, Daisy. You're all excited now.

Daisy: Even alone I can't say I never loved Tom. It wouldn't be true.

TOM: Of course it wouldn't!

DAISY *(to him)*: As if it mattered to you.

TOM: Of course it matters! I'm going to take better care of you from now on.

GATSBY: You don't understand. You're not going to take care of her any more. She is leaving you.

TOM: Nonsense.

DAISY: I am, though.

TOM: She's not leaving me. Certainly not for a common swindler who would have to steal the ring he put on her finger.

DAISY: I won't stand this. Nick! Take me home!

TOM: I've been making a little investigation of this man, you know — and I've found out quite a lot of things. I found out what your drug stores were.

(He turns to Nick)

He and this Wolfshiem bought up a lot of side street drug stores between here and Chicago and have been selling grain alcohol over the counter. That's one of his little stunts. I picked him for a big bootlegger the first time I ever saw him, and I wasn't far from wrong.

DAISY *(to Gatsby)*: Tell him it isn't true.

TOM: Oh, that's only a side line, but the Federal officers are onto it now, and that's gone, with all the rest.

GATSBY: He's telling half the truth and a mess of lies. Don't listen to him. What does it matter? What does it matter how I've made my money?

TOM: Your money! You haven't any money! The bank called your loan today, didn't it? You haven't made your second payment on this house here and tomorrow you'll be thrown out onto the road. You're not only a bluff and a common swindler but you're a crook, and you're going to jail!

DAISY: No!

TOM: The District Attorney is asking for his indictment before the grand jury for passing some forged bonds on a bank in New Jersey. Is that enough, or do you want to hear some more about the Great Gatsby?

DAISY: Take me home! I want to go home!

GATSBY: It doesn't matter what he says. Part of it's true — but it doesn't matter.

DAISY: Take me home, Tom!

GATSBY: What I did I had to do. I had to raise myself up to where you were. He lies when he says I can't take care of you. I have a few thousand here in my pocket. I've always kept that for you — I can get a new start, you shan't want for anything. Surely you know I'd never let you want for anything.

TOM: You're out of your class, old sport. You can't speak her language.

GATSBY: Daisy! Listen to —

(Myrtle runs in at back and through the window)

MYRTLE: Tom! Help me! He beat me! He —

(She runs to Tom)

TOM: Get away!

(He pushes her away roughly and she staggers to center. To prevent her from falling Gatsby throws out his arms and catches her. As he holds her for a moment in his arms there is a pistol shot from outside and he staggers back, his hand pressed to his side)

The confrontation between Wilson and Gatsby.

NICK: Gatsby!

(Wilson comes to the window with a revolver in his hand)

MYRTLE: You swine! You dirty swine!

(Wilson raises his revolver and fires — Myrtle falls at stage right, center. Wilson turns and runs out. Gatsby crosses slowly toward Daisy)

GATSBY: Daisy — Daisy.

(He falls at stage center)

JORDAN: Oh my God!

DAISY: Tom! Take me home! I don't want to be mixed up in this — take me home!

TOM: Yes — come!

NICK: He was the best of the whole damned crowd of us!

(He stands looking down at Gatsby)

DAISY: Take me home!

THE END

Spoof bookplate by illustrator Herb Roth.

ANNOTATIONS

5.8 "Over There" This patriotic song would have been familiar to most of the audience. It was written by George M. Cohan in 1917 to encourage young American men to enlist in the armed forces for World War I.

6.12 Camp Taylor This military base, located some six miles from downtown Louisville, was named for President Zachary Taylor. For a time it was the largest US Army training camp during the war. Fitzgerald, a second lieutenant in the infantry, was stationed at Camp Taylor in March and April 1918.

19.6 "Tipperary" "It's a Long Way to Tipperary," an Irish music-hall song dating from 1912, was a popular marching song for soldiers during World War I.

20.3 West Egg There is no place named West Egg or East Egg on Long Island. The two towns roughly correspond to Great Neck and Cow Neck (more commonly known as Manhasset Neck), New York. Both are situated on small "necks" of land in Long Island Sound, on the North Shore of the island itself. The "Eggs" were commuter towns for New York City by the 1920s.

25.8 Jordan Baker? Jordan's name would have brought to mind two sporty vehicles manufactured for women drivers — the Jordan Runabout and the Baker Electric. Both cars were two-seaters; both were manufactured in Cleveland, Ohio. In a 1924 letter to Max Perkins, Fitzgerald indicated that the champion golfer Edith Cummings (1899–1984), was his inspiration for Jordan Baker.

27.7 The man who fixed the World's Series Meyer Wolfshiem is based on the gambler and racketeer Arnold Rothstein (1882–1928), who was involved in the infamous "Black Sox" scandal in 1919. Several players from the Chicago White Sox accepted bribes to throw the World's Series that fall; eight of them, the "eight men out," including the legendary Joseph Jefferson "Shoeless Joe" Jackson, were permanently banned from baseball. Rothstein, who was alleged to be in on the fix, won more than $300,000 by betting on their opponents, the Cincinnati Reds. The conspiracy was exposed, but Rothstein was not charged with wrongdoing. Rothstein was murdered in 1928 over a gambling debt.

33.3 Goddard Tom is thinking of the historian and eugenicist Lothrop Stoddard (1883–1950), author of *The Rising Tide of Color: The Threat Against White World-Supremacy* (1920). Stoddard predicted a racial world war if Asians and Africans were not prevented from migrating to Western countries.

39.2 Scott has been with me for years Davis added this unseen, offstage character as Tom Buchanan's valet or butler, and gave him Fitzgerald's name.

44.23 It looks like the World's Fair World's fairs, also called international expositions, have been held globally since the mid-nineteenth century to celebrate industrialization, the arts, technological advances, and national image. The most recent ones to have been held in the United States in 1926 were in 1904 (the Louisiana Purchase Exposition, St. Louis) and in 1915 (the Panama-Pacific Exposition, San Francisco).

45.12 The Argonne battles The Meuse-Argonne offensive began in September 1918 and was concluded only by the armistice ending World War I. American troops suffered heavy losses.

48.6 or even worse in Atlanta Wolfshiem means the federal penitentiary in Atlanta, Georgia, completed in 1902. This prison housed 1,200 inmates.

48.21 welcher … stool Ryan is warning Gatsby that Blakely is a swindler or scammer who does not pay his debts, and who has been a police informer or "stool pigeon."

49.18 Rosey Rosenthal Wolfshiem is recounting an actual event here. Early in the morning of July 16, 1912, the gambler Herman "Rosy" Rosenthal left the Hotel Metropole, near Times Square. Four men waiting outside shot and killed Rosenthal. They were arrested, found guilty of murder, and sent to the electric chair at the Sing Sing Correctional Facility in Ossining, New York. New York Police Department lieutenant Charles Becker, who had paid Rosenthal's killers, was also given the death penalty.

54.2 Von Hindenburg Paul von Hindenburg (1847–1934) was field marshal of the German forces during World War I. From 1925 until 1934 he served as president of Germany.

54.29 little movie star … with wonderful red hair Davis is surely implying here that Clara Bow, the "It" girl, is a guest at Gatsby's party. Clara Gordon Bow (1905–1965) was born in Brooklyn and by the mid-1920s was a major movie star, best known for her vivacity, sex appeal, and (even in the days of black and white film) her tangle of bobbed copper curls. In 1924, Bow created a sensation in *Grit*, a movie about teenage criminals with a screenplay by Fitzgerald. *Red Hair* (1928) featured a brief, glorious burst of Bow in Technicolor.

59.7 Beefsteak Charlie's Charles Chessar, a New York restaurateur nicknamed "Beefsteak Charlie," moved his increasingly popular restaurant to 216 West 50th Street in 1914. Beefsteak Charlie's was a favorite spot for athletes and sports fans until it closed in 1934. The house specialty was a steak sandwich.

66.16 Belasco David Belasco (1853–1931) was a Broadway dramatist, producer, and director known especially for creating realistic illusions onstage.

67.19 the bathing beauties Producer Mack Sennett (1880–1960), the "King of Comedy," assembled a group of young women, dressed them in bathing suits, and filmed them in short comic movies from 1915 through the 1920s. Alumna who were "Sennett Bathing Beauties" in their early days included the actresses Mabel Normand, Gloria Swanson, and Carole Lombard.

94.14 Kapiolani ... the Punch Bowl Kapiolani is a public park above Waikiki Beach in Honolulu, on Oahu in the Hawaiian Islands. The crater of an extinct volcano in Honolulu, about an hour's walk from Kapiolani, is popularly known as "the Punch Bowl."